AURA WEAVING

Interpreting and Activating Energy Fields

AURA WEAVING

Dr. Charlie Watts & Judah Andrews,
the Founders of Aura Weaver

STERLING ETHOS
New York

STERLING ETHOS and the distinctive Sterling Ethos logo are registered trademarks of Sterling Publishing Co., Inc.

Text © 2025 Charlie Watts and Judah Andrews

All rights reserved. No part of this publication may be reproduced, stored in a retrieval system, or transmitted in any form or by any means (including electronic, mechanical, photocopying, recording, or otherwise) without prior written permission from the publisher.

ISBN 978-1-4549-5633-4
ISBN 978-1-4549-5634-1 (e-book)

Library of Congress Control Number: 2024950030

For information about custom editions, special sales, and premium purchases, please contact specialsales@unionsquareandco.com.

Printed in Malaysia

2 4 6 8 10 9 7 5 3 1

unionsquareandco.com

Cover and interior design by Erik Jacobsen
Cover images courtesy of authors (aura); by AlyonaZhitnaya/Shutterstock.com (stars)
Interior images courtesy of authors, except art on p. v by Maggie Boyd;
courtesy of Library of Congress: 61

To our mamas, Cynthia and Ronnie, who always encouraged us to believe we could do anything with our lives. While this probably isn't what they had in mind, we're forever grateful they embraced our weirdness along the way. Love you both to the moon and back!

INTRODUCTION 1

PART 1. THE AURA

CHAPTER 1
The Aura: Our Luminous Energy Egg 11

CHAPTER 2
Developing Cosmic Sight: How to See an Aura 41

CHAPTER 3
A Brief History of Aura Photography 53

CHAPTER 4
Read the Rainbow: How to Interpret an Aura 71

CHAPTER 5
Aura Archetypes 91

PART 2. AURA WEAVING

CHAPTER 6
Aura Weaving 101 **127**

CHAPTER 7
Channeling **139**

CHAPTER 8
Spider Woman: Weaving Aura Power **171**

CHAPTER 9
Advanced Aura Magick **187**

CONCLUSION 210
FURTHER READING 212
ACKNOWLEDGMENTS 213
ABOUT THE AUTHORS 214

INTRODUCTION

You may hesitate to consider yourself a practitioner of magic. You might perceive the understanding and manipulation of auras as something extraordinary or beyond your capabilities—a realm reserved for the special few who are born with these esoteric gifts. This is simply not true.

You are more than just your meat suit. You are woven from stardust, cradled on a celestial rock hurtling through the cosmos. You are brimming with magic. What better way to understand this magic than by exploring the luminous tapestry of your aura?

In the following pages, you will embark on a journey into the mystical world of auras, guided by our two experiences, as well as the knowledge we've accumulated from decades of photographing and analyzing the auras of tens of thousands of people. This book bridges the gap between esoteric knowledge and practical application, making the realm of auras accessible to all. Whether you are a seasoned spiritual practitioner or a curious beginner, you will gain profound insights into the colors and layers of your aura, enhancing your relationship to your energy and life's purpose. Through guided exercises, meditations, and personal anecdotes, you will learn to balance and harmonize your aura, unlocking its power for manifestation, creativity, and healing. By recognizing and utilizing the energetic patterns in your aura, you can attract abundance and more deeply understand your unique purpose for this life. Our auras provide a blueprint of our souls; understanding that allows you to more fully understand yourself.

Auras are the place where art, magic, and science collide, offering a unique perspective on our interconnected existence. This book connects you to ancient traditions and modern insights, offering a rich history of knowledge that fosters deeper connections with yourself and others. By understanding and cocreating with your aura, you will lead a more purposeful and harmonious life.

Aura Weaving, at its essence, is an energy healing modality that invites you to connect deeply and fully with yourself by understanding the intricate layers of your aura. To help you grasp the concepts and practice of Aura Weaving, this book is divided into two parts. The first part delves into the nature of the aura—its history, how it has been interpreted over time, and the way we see it today through the lens of aura photography. You will explore the archetypes, colors, and their positioning within the aura, as well as how these elements have been decoded across different cultures and practices.

The second part of the book is an invitation for you to step into the flow of your own energy field, using this ancient wisdom to engage with your aura in a way that fully empowers your life. This is not about divination in the traditional sense of fortune-telling, but rather a tool for deeper self-understanding. By knowing your aura, you gain insight into the unique threads of your journey, the energies surrounding you, and how they weave together to form the tapestry of your life's purpose. This practice allows you to see the present more clearly, embody your mission for this incarnation, and consciously manifest your path by aligning with the universe's flow. Aura Weaving

is both a new and timeless practice, one that we are cocreating with the cosmos—and with you—in this present moment.

Below are our personal introductions, giving you an idea of how this fascinating subject has shaped our respective lives. We'll share more throughout the book in hope of giving the readers more perspective on how to cultivate an awareness of auras and use it to improve their relationships to both the material and the spiritual worlds.

Charlie

The day my family piled into a canoe to drift down a small, winding river, I was filled with an eagerness to keep pace with the others, paddling with all my might. As we rounded a sharp bend, the canoe struck a hidden rock and flipped, catapulting me into the frigid water. The shock of the cold was a sudden, bracing reminder of nature's unpredictable power, a baptism into the wild, fluid dance of the river. The current surged around me, pushing me down, until disorientation and panic set in. I flailed desperately, but the water claimed me, dragging me deeper and deeper. On the riverbed, I became ensnared in the branches of a submerged tree, my head and neck trapped. Water filled my lungs as I struggled for breath, trapped and running out of air. Then suddenly, something changed: a sense of being in a different place washed over me, a feeling of detachment that transcended my immediate peril. A bright light opened before me, revealing a glowing, underground tunnel that seemed to exist both beneath and above me simultaneously, as if split by a mirror. On the other side of the light, a group of familiar figures beckoned me, their presence both comforting and enigmatic, inviting me to step beyond the confines of the present moment.

Terrified at first, I didn't understand what was happening or where these figures wanted me to go. Yet I felt like I had always known them. A sense of trust and surrender enveloped me, as if a greater force was guiding me to a safe path. The figures were beautiful and luminescent, pure and radiant, filling my being. Their forms shifted and shimmered like shadows. They seemed so familiar, yet strange.

Then they posed a question that would chart the course of my life: Did I want to come with them now, or did I choose to come later? In that suspended moment, I felt a profound connection to the universe, sensing that I was more than just an individual—I was part of a vast, interconnected whole—a spiderweb that intertwined everything to me and me to everything. The awareness of my ten-year-old self crystallized, and I knew I wasn't ready to leave this world just yet. With a deep sense of resolve and purpose, I made my choice. I chose to stay.

At that moment, one of the adults in the canoe reached into the water and pulled me out. I gasped for air, then vomited. And as I returned to myself, a raw, new energy coursed through me. This experience had unlocked a hidden door deep within, releasing a latent spiritual knowledge. I now possessed the ability to sense and see auras. Over time, I learned to create with this power, delving deeper into my mystical journey and understanding the true beauty and mystery of the universe through auras and our connection to the energy that surrounds us all.

The colors of the aura became a language that spoke to me, revealing the emotional, mental, and spiritual states of those around me. At first I was hesitant to share this newfound knowledge, afraid of how others might judge me. I pursued the unholy trinity of alcohol, drugs, and sex in a desperate attempt to dim these overwhelming powers. But as I grew older and my understanding and confidence grew, I began to see and value the power and potential of this gift. It was a delicate dance with the unseen, a symphony of colors and energies that wove together my existence, inviting me to listen and learn, to embrace and share.

Through my exploration of auras, I have come to connect with people in wondrous new ways and ended my own sixteen-year-long battle with addiction. I've begun to recognize the struggles and challenges others face, as well as the beauty and radiance within them. By sharing my knowledge, I've helped others unlock their own unique spiritual power, see the world with new eyes, and find a deeper sense of meaning and purpose.

In this book, written with my husband, Judah Andrews, we invite you into the mystical world of auras—a realm of wonder, mystery, and beauty. Allow this book to guide you in unveiling the intricate practice of Aura Weaving, a metaphysical art centered on cocreation, balancing, and harmonizing the aura. Through Aura Weaving I have found my life's purpose of being a Root Chakra warrior as a pelvic floor occupational therapist and energy healer. I hope this process does the same for you.

Through our experiences and those of others, and the great gift of having read over five thousand auras personally and photographing thirty thousand auras through my company, Aura Weaver, I hope to guide you toward an understanding of this gift's true power and inspire you to

weave your own threads into the infinite spiderweb of interconnectedness, embracing the energy that binds us all in its luminous embrace.

Judah

The message from my Christian church was clear: The supernatural is real. There are ghosts, spirits, and unseen forces. We battle not flesh and blood but the spirit. Jesus is the champion defending your soul from annihilation or eternal torture. I was about nine when I grasped this horrifying concept.

Returning from a church function, I fell asleep in the back seat of the car. A pothole jolted me awake. I was still in a hypnagogic state, and my brain incorporated the visuals of the encroaching dusk of the landscape around me into the end of a vanishing dream. There was a moment when the dream and what my eyes were seeing were the same thing. I asked my mother, "Mom, how do you know what's real?" She replied, "Sweetheart, THIS is real." Content with her tone, the question was buried, only to resurface years later during my first experiences with psychedelics.

In my teens, I was further programmed by ethno-religious interpretations of modern texts, dictating how to vote and whom to marry. These texts were promoted as infallible, and competing ideas were deemed heretical. The fear of eternal consequences was paralyzing, despite being reminded I had a "free" choice. Oh, the countless ways you could find your way to hell.

Having this existential gun to my head made me feel powerless, although I was constantly reminded by both community and clergy that I had a "free" choice—a choice that comes with eternal consequences and no do-overs.

The pulpit framed the world as fallen and impure. Many in my church seemed unwavering in their conviction. I, however, was plagued by the contradiction of how one could know the truth with a broken mind.

I became an agent for Christ, driven by fear and communal acceptance. Suppressing desires and denying impulses stunted the growth of my personality. I chastised those who didn't conform. I reminded gay people they were going to hell.

In my late teens, doubts remained despite my comprehensively Christian household. I was told these doubts were external manifestations. Once, after ignoring my father's request to clean my room, he found a book of ghost stories. I was punished, and my hide was "tanned" for possessing occult contraband. The spanking hurt, but honestly I was more bummed about losing that cool book of scary ghost stories.

Years of confusion and conflicting realities fueled my rage. I hadn't taken responsibility for my anger and shame about my emerging sexual nature and curiosity. These were issues not my own, but a product of the fallen nature of the world. It felt easy to distance myself from impulsiveness. I became a witness and purveyor to suffering. The instinctual feeling to help those in need, question authority, and express my mind became steadily eroded by cultural, religious, and racial ambiguities.

The reckoning of my doubt leached away my inspirations and creativity. My anxiety culminated in a serious bout with panic attacks, leading to an unsustainable reliance on drugs. In the tireless quest for relief, an online search led me to *Way of the Peaceful Warrior* by Dan Millman. Upon completing that book, I never had another panic attack. The story had transmuted my anxiety through narrative and symbolic alchemy, and I emerged deeply intrigued by this personal transformation, which I experienced practically overnight.

My mind and my heart could never settle on atheism. Nor could I reconcile the purpose of existence through purely physical and scientific means. I realized those tools were inadequate for comprehending something so vast and immaterial. Symbols and feelings held significance that couldn't be quantified by conventional science—only by the mind of a thinking, feeling human. It became clear to me that while orthodox science demands repeatable evidence, the world of metaphysics requires a different lens—one with intuition and perception as vital elements of truth. Instead of adopting a religion, I became committed to the lifelong process of self-discovery. When I met Charlie, she opened my eyes to the path of the serious student in esoterica. I would still have my doubts, and relapse into dogmatic thinking from time to time, but through the world of alchemical symbology, I had finally found a way to nourish the seeker within. As my journey unfolded, I found value in exploring diverse philosophies and practices. I delved into mindfulness meditation with the guidance of David Nichtern of Dharma Moon in a sangha, which helped me learn how to become a gentle observer of my thoughts. The grounding nature of this practice among others allowed me to bridge the gap between metaphysics and my inherited faith. Eventually, even my estrangement from the Christian Bible began to fade. I discovered that this ancient text was filled with powerful esoteric symbology and wisdom. It took years of philosophical study to detangle the dogmatic and colonial programming to better understand the teaching of the Bible—a process that continues to this day.

Without much trouble, the connections between the different pieces of my spiritual exploration began to alchemize. Every disparate anecdote, scientific discovery, and conflicting scripture could exist within a paradigm of understanding the self. Then one day I got an aura photo. I can't say that moment was life-changing, but it planted the seed that grew into a realization that spirit and material collided in some measurable way. Aura photography stood out as one of the most accessible ways to engage people in meaningful, intuitive conversations and enrich this process of self-discovery and transformation. After many aura photos and profound experiences from sharing the technology with other people, I gave myself permission to treat my intuition as a real thing. The years that followed that choice were in fact life-changing. The skeptic inside me evolved into an organizer of experience and perception. I believe the empathic and intuitive powers of the world's people are desperately needed. This book is our contribution to that effort. We hope there is something here that touches your heart.

PART 1:
THE AURA

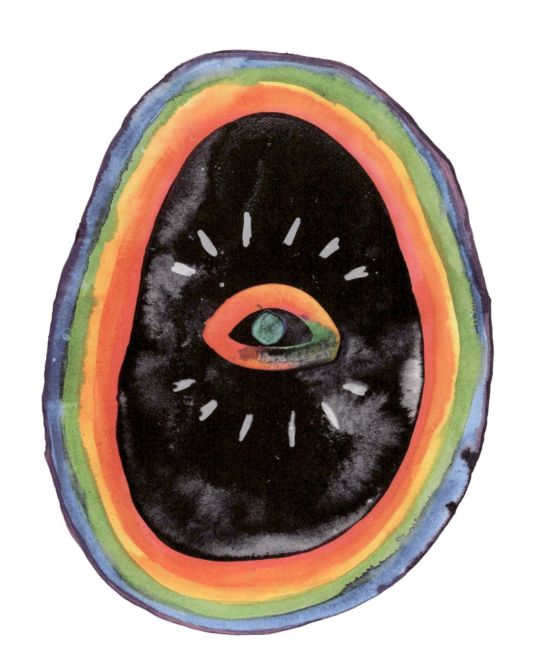

CHAPTER 1

The Aura: Our Luminous Energy Egg

The aura is an invisible, ethereal energy field that envelops and penetrates us all, mirroring the multifaceted layers of our inner selves. A holy onion of many-colored layers, this luminous flame, unseen by the naked eye, is a canvas where our emotions and experiences paint their stories and embolden our creativity. Whether it blazes with vibrant hues of joy and vitality or is muddied with the somber shades of fear and sadness, the aura offers a profound glimpse into the human psyche.

Throughout history, mystics, priests, sages, monks, witches, and spiritual practitioners have sought to understand and harness the aura's power, recognizing its vital role in shaping our experiences and interactions with the world. In the Hindu scriptures, dating back to around 800 BCE, the Upanishads speak of the Prana, a life-force energy that surrounds and permeates all living things. Similarly, ancient Buddhist texts from the fifth century BCE describe the Pāli Canon, which mentions luminous auras as manifestations of one's spiritual state. In Christian iconography, dating from the fourth century CE, saints are often depicted with radiant halos, signifying divine presence and holiness. These ancient texts speak through a timeless understanding that our essence extends beyond the physical—that we are more than our bodies.

In its simplest form, the human aura is an "energy egg," with the physical body as its yolk. Our thoughts, emotions, and experiences ripple through the body and are reflected in the aura. This field is constantly broadcasting and receiving energy, a nebulous dance of impulses from the mind and body. The aura is an antenna picking up on both the world around us and our inner state.

The aura acts as a barometer, offering invaluable feedback on the emotional and energetic state of our vessel. By attuning to the subtle vibrations of our aura, we can uncover the underlying disharmony or disconnection we may feel and take steps toward healing.

The aura serves as a mirror, reflecting the raw truth of who we are beyond the masks and facades we present to the world. It invites us to embrace our authenticity fully and unapologetically, to trust in the wisdom of our inner guidance, and to honor the innate intelligence of our energetic being. The aura is an untapped wellspring of power for manifestation. This book will illuminate the path and act as a meditation to connect you more fully with your aura.

We first learned of the luminous egg from our teacher, *curandero*, and beloved friend Alberto Roman—a most magical human. He has brought infinite wisdom and silliness into our lives. He offers the following message below on the luminous egg:

> This is what I can offer you about the luminous egg. You see, in ceremony, embodiment of the luminous egg often arises spontaneously, shaped by the particular horizon of meaning we're standing on in that moment of the ceremony. My understanding of the luminous egg comes from three traditions that have woven themselves into my work. One is the Dogon egg from Africa, a symbol of self-fertilizing matter, the spark of life that gives rise to form. Then there's the tantric egg, carrying a similar thread of creation, and finally, the luminosity of the Mesoamerican traditions, where our light egg becomes the fabric of our very being.
>
> When I bring the luminous egg into ceremony, it's usually toward the end, when the energy has ripened and we're ready to gather all the colors, all the vibrations we've touched on, and create a protective, sovereign space around ourselves. I often guide people to sit on their thrones within this egg—totally at ease, fully inhabiting their own light. It's not just about shielding, but about being in the center of your own energy, fully present with everything that shows up.
>
> There's a practice I suggest when you find yourself in situations of discomfort or danger. You bring your palms together, over your head, and then bring them down, tracing the shape of an egg around your body. This motion draws the aura into the form of a luminous egg, an energetic boundary. But remember, this egg is permeable. It doesn't shut you off from the world—rather, it interacts with the environment, knowing that the self is constantly shaped by what's around us.
>
> In these traditions, the source of who we are is not separate from our surroundings. The luminous egg teaches us this: knowing the world is a way of knowing ourselves. And with that, I hope this gives you some direction. If more questions arise, you'll know where to go from here—because this unfolding, this energy, is intelligent. Trust in the luminous egg; it will guide you.

Aura Anatomy

To truly understand the nature of the aura, we must explore its layers and colors, its constantly shifting state, and the chakras—those vital energy centers within the body that both influence and are influenced by the aura. The aura, an omnipresent force, is an electromagnetic field of vibrant light that wraps around our form. It serves as both a shield and bridge, linking us to the world around us and to the deeper parts of our own being.

As we proceed, we'll delve into the subtle power of each chakra and aura layer through meditation. This book includes exercises to help you sense and guide these energies, to feel and understand the ebb and flow within these vibrational fields.

By working through the exercises on color, we connect with each energy center, building a bond and deeper sense of self. Our aim is not to perfect the aura's hues but to see our current state, its lessons, and our place within the larger scheme. What would you do with this new self-awareness?

The Chakras

In order to understand the aura, we must first look to chakras, an ancient system of understanding the concentration of energy in the body, originating in Hinduism. Chakras are vital energy centers within the human body, sometime referred to as wheels, serving as nodes for the reception, assimilation, and transmission of life energies. Each chakra is traditionally associated with specific bodily functions, psychological attributes, and spiritual dimensions. Their alignment and balance significantly impact one's overall well-being, influencing everything from emotional responses to physical health. Chakras are intrinsically linked to the aura, contributing to its layers with unique vibrations and colors. When chakras are open and aligned, the aura radiates more brightly, with clearer colors reflecting an individual's health and spiritual state. Conversely, blockages or imbalances in the chakras manifest as disturbances or dullness in the corresponding regions of the aura. Understanding and working with chakras can provide profound insights into the functioning of the aura, offering pathways to holistic healing and energetic harmony.

Chakras are often visualized not only as simple energy centers but as dynamic, spinning vortexes of energy within the body, like spirals or wheels. This spiral motion is crucial, representing the way chakras draw in and channel universal life force into both physical and subtle, or energetic, bodies. Each chakra spins at its own frequency, and the nature of this spinning is integral to how effectively it functions.

The spiral movement of a chakra aids the flow of energy in and out the aura. When chakras spin smoothly and at balanced rates, they maintain equilibrium in the energy flow, essential for optimal physical, mental, and emotional health. A well-functioning chakra spiral acts like a pump, pulling in energy from the environment to nourish the body and expelling stale or unneeded energy. Spirals also reflect the dynamic and ever-changing nature of our energy centers. Just as spirals can expand and contract, so too can the chakras adjust their activity levels based on our physical condition, emotional states, and spiritual growth. The ability of the chakras to modulate their spinning, influenced by internal and external factors, underscores their complex role in our energy anatomy.

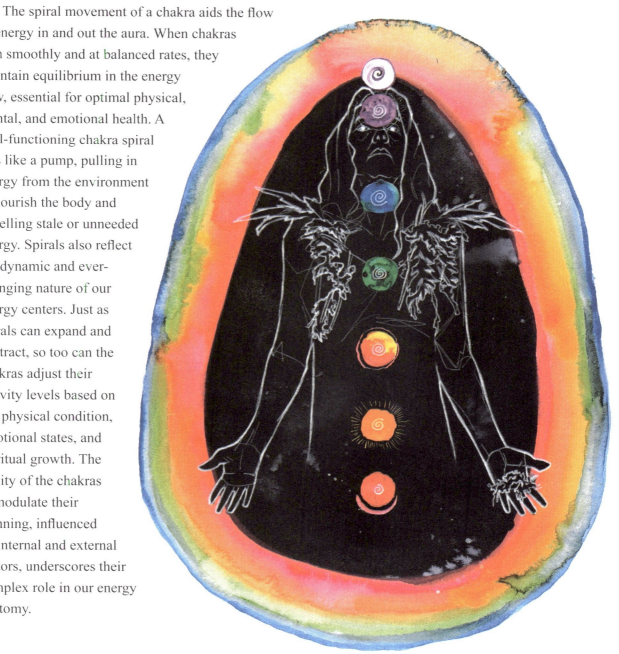

Root Chakra

The Root Chakra, also known as the Base Chakra, is where our sense of security and survival resides. Visualize the color red to feel its grounding energy, anchoring yourself to the present moment.

Sacral Chakra

We then ascend to the Sacral Chakra, the center of our creativity and sexuality. Here the vibrant orange hues inspire discussions about passion, pleasure, and the birthing of new ideas.

Solar Plexus Chakra

The Solar Plexus Chakra, radiating bright yellow, invites us to explore our personal power, self-esteem, and the joy of being. It's a reminder of the inner sun that shines within each of us, the source of our inner strength and confidence.

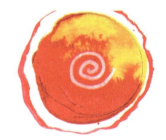

Heart Chakra

As we reach the Heart Chakra, enveloped in lush green, we talk about love—not just romantic love, but the universal love that connects us all. It's in this space that we often feel the most profound shifts, as if our hearts are opening up to a deeper understanding of ourselves and others.

Throat Chakra

The Throat Chakra, with its soothing blue energy, challenges us to communicate our truth, to express ourselves authentically and listen with equal openness. We practice vocal exercises, feeling the vibration of our voices as they resonate with this energy center.

Third Eye Chakra

Our journey takes us upward to the Third Eye Chakra, a realm of intuition, insight, and inner vision. Here the indigo light invites us to trust our inner guidance, to see beyond the physical realm into the realm of deeper knowing.

Crown Chakra

Finally we reach the Crown Chakra, where a sense of spiritual connection and oneness with the universe prevails. Here envision a brilliant white light, a cosmic connection that binds us to the infinite.

Mapping the Chakras in the Body

Behind each category of chakra are the physical organs of which they're made. Each organ of the human body not only performs its physiological functions but also possesses a unique energetic signature that contributes to the layers of the aura. In short, the chakras power the aura. This concept suggests that the health and vibrancy of an individual's aura can be directly influenced by the health and balance of their internal organs. Here's a closer look at how this energetic interplay functions and its implications for overall well-being.

Each organ in the body is thought to emit its own specific type of energy, which reflects its state of health and its functional importance in the body's ecosystem. These energies contribute to layers of the aura. Disturbances in an organ are believed to manifest as distortions or discolorations in the corresponding areas of the aura.

The Heart

Often associated with the color green in aura readings, the heart's energy is connected to emotions of love and compassion. A vibrant, clear green around the chest area in the aura can indicate a healthy heart, both physically and emotionally, while a muddied green might suggest heart-related ailments or emotional distress.

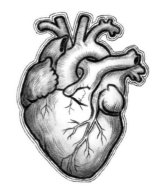

The Liver

Typically linked with the color yellow, which corresponds to the Solar Plexus Chakra, the liver's energy reflects issues of anger, frustration, and general vitality. A bright and pure yellow in the aura can suggest a healthy and well-functioning liver, whereas a dull or cloudy yellow might indicate liver stress or dysfunction.

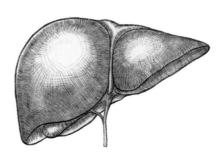

The Kidneys

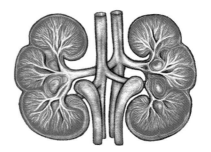

According to traditional Chinese medicine, the kidneys are the reservoir of our life force or qi, which is essential for vitality and longevity. They are often associated with the color blue and are linked to the Root and Sacral Chakras. The kidneys hold energy related to fear and survival instincts, with healthy kidneys indicated by a clear blue aura, suggesting a balanced approach to fear and stress. Conversely, a gray or murky blue could suggest adrenal fatigue or chronic fear, reflecting an imbalance in these foundational energies.

Aura Layers

An aura is a collection of ethereal layers surrounding us. Each layer, like a delicate sheath, holds its own unique significance and story. These layers, often visualized as concentric bands of energy around the body, represent different aspects of an individual's well-being, from the Etheric Layer, which is nearest to the flesh and tied to health and physical sensations, to the outer Spiritual Layers linking us to universal energies and higher states of mind. Together these layers form a complex system, reflecting and influencing one's physical, emotional, mental, and spiritual health.

There are many systems used when discussing aura layers. We use Charles Webster Leadbeater's foundational structure. An influential theosophist in the early twentieth century, he pioneered the exploration of aura layers, integrating his observations with theosophical teachings to define the subtle bodies and their interactions. Then, in the late twentieth century, Barbara Brennan, a former NASA physicist turned healer, expanded upon these foundations in her seminal work, *Hands of Light*, offering a detailed, structured system of the aura layers, combining scientific insight with metaphysical knowledge.

Starting closest to the body is the Etheric Layer, which extends approximately one to three inches away. It is tightly linked to our physical health and vitality, resonating closely with the Root Chakra, which governs our foundational instincts and our sense of grounding and security. This layer acts almost as a ghostly twin, mirroring the physical body's state.

Just beyond the Etheric, we find the Emotional Layer, stretching two to four inches from the body. Governed by the Sacral Chakra, this vibrant layer is where our emotions flow freely, displaying the dynamic spectrum of our feelings, from joy and love to sorrow and fear. This layer teaches us about the transient nature of emotions, reminding us that, like waves, they come and go, influencing our energy with their intensity and hues.

The Mental Layer sits three to eight inches from the physical body and is associated with the Solar Plexus Chakra. It encompasses our beliefs, thoughts, and mental actions, representing the structured yet fluid realm where our cognitive processes mold our aura's energy. This layer is where our mental discipline and the power of our convictions shape our overall energy field, influencing both our inner balance and our external interactions.

Progressing outward, about one foot from the body, is the Astral Layer. This layer serves as a bridge between the tangible world and the spiritual realms, and is deeply connected with the Heart Chakra. Here our personal relationships and emotional bonds extend into the collective, blending our personal love and compassion with universal energies.

Two feet away from the body lies the Etheric Template Layer, aligned with the Throat Chakra. This layer holds the template or blueprint for the Etheric Layer, representing our true expression and higher will. It serves as a mold for the etheric structure, providing a higher spiritual framework for our physical existence.

Lastly, the Celestial/Causal Layer, extending two and a half feet from the body and linked with the Third Eye Chakra, signifies the onset of our deep spiritual connections. It encompasses our intuition and our capacity for spiritual reflection, marking the space where we begin to understand our place within the universe and the deeper meanings of our life experiences.

Each layer of the aura can dynamically contract and expand, much like the rhythm of breath, influenced by a person's emotional state, health, and spiritual well-being. These fluctuations are not fixed and can vary widely depending on numerous factors, including a person's mental, emotional, and physical state at any given time. For example, during meditation or intense spiritual practice, the layers of the aura might expand significantly, indicating a heightened state of consciousness and openness. Conversely, during times of stress, feeling unsafe, or illness, the aura may contract, becoming smaller and less vibrant.

This dynamic nature of the aura is beautifully illustrated by the story of a Buddha, whose aura was said to extend for miles. According to legend, this Buddha, through years of dedicated spiritual practice and profound compassion, had developed an aura so powerful and expansive that it could be felt across vast distances, enveloping the surrounding area with a sense of peace and enlightenment. This story exemplifies the potential of human spiritual growth and the extraordinary impact that such an expansive aura can have not only on the individual but also on the broader environment.

1 The Etheric Layer

The Etheric Layer is the closest whisper of light tethering us to the material world, like the soft hum of a newborn star. It hovers just beyond the skin, holding the essence of our physical body, mirroring our vitality. Linked to the Root Chakra, this layer pulses with the rhythm of survival, grounding us in the present moment, and anchoring our spirit to the earth. Here the physical and energetic worlds touch, and the body finds its first home in the luminous egg.

- Closest to the physical body
- Extending one to three inches from the body
- Associated with the Root Chakra

2 The Emotional Layer

Like the gentle swell of the ocean, the Emotional Layer flows just beyond the Etheric. It holds our shifting emotional tides—joy, sorrow, love, and fear—encapsulating the raw, vivid colors of our emotional landscape. Governed by the Sacral Chakra, this layer moves with the rhythm of our feelings, reminding us that emotion is a living current, one that shapes and reshapes our energetic form with every experience, every tear, and every laughter.

- Directly outside the etheric layer
- Approximately two to four inches away from the physical body
- Associated with the Sacral Chakra
- Holds all our emotions and feelings, such as joy, sorrow, love, and hate

3 The Mental Layer

In the golden embrace of the Mental Layer, thought takes shape as form. This is where our intellectual processes live—rules, beliefs, judgments, and the architecture of our mental world. Aligned with the Solar Plexus Chakra, this layer illuminates the mind's order, tracing the patterns of our self-perception and the thoughts that create our reality. Here clarity of intention shapes the threads of our aura, weaving them into a coherent narrative.

- Three to eight inches from the physical body
- Associated with the Solar Plexus Chakra
- Governs mental thought processes such as rules, regulations, judgment, and discipline

4 The Astral Layer

The Astral Layer acts as a bridge between worlds—a meeting point between the earthly and the spiritual. It radiates from the Heart Chakra, vibrating with love that transcends the self, connecting us to the collective heartbeat of humanity. In this space, we feel the expansiveness of connection, where personal relationships become threads in the vast web of universal love and compassion. It is here that the personal dissolves into the collective.

- One foot from the physical body
- Bridge between the lower vibrations of the physical plane and the higher vibrations of the spiritual

5 The Etheric Template

The Etheric Template is the blueprint of our energy, shaping the form of our aura and the patterns we carry. Linked to the Throat Chakra, this layer guides us in expressing our truest voice, aligning our speech and self-expression with the higher spiritual patterns. This is where we mold our etheric form, reflecting the purity of thought into the world. It is the mold from which we shape our etheric body and weave our narrative into the world.

- Two feet from the physical body
- Associated with the Throat Chakra

6 The Celestial/Causal Layer

The Celestial Layer is the dawning of spiritual insight, where intuition sharpens into wisdom. Connected to the Third Eye Chakra, this layer holds the spark of divine connection, the vision that transcends physical sight. It is here that we see the luminous threads of our soul's journey, glimpsing the patterns that weave our existence into the cosmic tapestry. The wisdom here is deep, still, and all-encompassing, offering clarity of purpose and sight beyond sight.

- Two and a half feet from the physical body
- Associated with the Third Eye Chakra
- This is where your spiritual connection begins

7 The Spiritual Layer

The outermost layer, the Spiritual Layer, radiates with the brilliance of pure light. It is the guardian of all layers, vibrating with the highest frequency and aligned with the Crown Chakra. This layer serves as our direct connection to the infinite, the divine, and the cosmos itself. It shields, protects, and completes our energetic form, bathing us in the golden glow of universal love and enlightenment.

- Three feet from the physical body
- Associated with the Crown Chakra
- Protects all the other layers
- Vibrates at the highest frequency
- Often seen as a brilliant white or golden light

These layers are not simply concepts but are living, breathing aspects of our being. Later in the book, we will practice sensing these layers, moving our hands through the air, feeling for the subtle shifts in energy. Some students are amazed when they feel a tangible resistance or warmth as they pass through these invisible fields.

Aura Colors

The colors captured in an aura resonate with the hues of the chakras, but with one profound distinction: they embody the human experience in motion. The color meanings described below are shaped by countless conversations with clients and our own personal journeys, reflecting the dynamic interplay of our lived realities and the energies that surround us.

Understanding the colors of the aura is akin to learning the secret language of the soul. Each hue speaks of stories of our innermost emotions, our struggles, and our triumphs. The vibrant spectrum of the aura serves as a bridge between our physical existence and the unseen energies that shape our reality. By attuning to these colors, we gain profound insight into our own essence and the interconnected web of life that binds us all. This chromatic symphony reveals not only who we are but also who we might become, inviting us to embrace the full spectrum of our being with curiosity and wonder.

Red is the beginning of your journey. Associated with the Root Chakra, red is the base color of our energy centers. It is also at the base of Maslow's hierarchy of needs, the physiological layer that concerns the basic primal needs for food, sex, and clothing. Red keeps you safe and in your body. When the body is stressed or traumatized, you might dissociate and leave or numb the human experience, but red pulls you back into the body to help keep you present and grounded. It is essentially the weighted blanket of aura colors.

In color psychology, red is known for its intense and stimulating effects. It increases heart rate, evokes strong emotions, and can even enhance physical reactions, such as appetite and alertness. This is why many fast-food restaurants use red in their logos; it subtly encourages hunger and quick decision-making.

In aura readings, a vibrant red aura is often interpreted as a sign of a strong-willed and energetic individual, someone with a robust sense of self and a readiness to take on challenges. A muddied or dark red aura, however, might indicate unresolved anger or frustration, suggesting a need for grounding and balance.

From a physics standpoint, red is the longest wavelength of visible light, around 620 to 750 nanometers. This longer wavelength means red light has a lower frequency and vibrates less than other colors in the visible spectrum. This slower vibration resonates with the Root Chakra's grounding qualities, anchoring us to the earth and our physical existence.

When starting a new project, forging a new relationship, or getting to know yourself better, red is the step back before the leap forward. It prepares you for all the challenges you need to face and helps ground you in the present moment. Red gets you grounded and then gets you going!

Orange is the color of raw creativity and manifestation. Associated with your Sacral Chakra, where the sex organs are located, it is the literal and figurative place of birth. Orange allows you to create something from nothing—to pull ideas from your imagination and bring them to life on Earth.

In color psychology, orange is known for its stimulating and enthusiastic qualities. It encourages socialization, joy, and a sense of adventure. The vibrant energy of orange can uplift your mood and inspire spontaneous and lively interactions. However, because orange exists in the emotional layer, it can carry an energy where negativity can easily get stuck. Emotional memories, especially those tied to past traumas or intense feelings, can linger in this layer, affecting your current emotional state.

In aura readings, a bright orange aura is often interpreted as a sign of someone who is passionate, creative, and full of life. This person likely has a strong drive to express themselves and manifest their desires. Conversely, a murky or dull orange aura might indicate emotional blockages or unresolved issues, suggesting a need to release these negative energies and restore balance.

Orange light has a wavelength between 590 and 620 nanometers. This intermediate wavelength, with its moderate frequency, resonates with the Sacral Chakra's qualities of fluidity and creativity, bridging the gap between the grounding energy of red and the stimulating energy of yellow.

The recollection of something from long ago can make you instantly angry because that emotional memory is stuck in the emotional layer of your aura. By working with the energy of orange, you can help release these trapped emotions, allowing for healing and the free flow of creative energy.

YELLOW

Yellow is sunshine, a sunflower blooming, a kid giggling. It brings joy and optimism into the auric field. Because of yellow's resonance with joy, it also is a powerful ally to abundance. Associated with digestion, yellow reminds you that happy gut health can help with happy mental health. Yellow is a confident color and one of the most extroverted of aura colors.

In color psychology, yellow is known to stimulate mental activity, generate muscle energy, and evoke cheerfulness. It's often linked to intellect and clarity, promoting creativity and original thought. However, its brightness can sometimes be overwhelming, reflecting the fine line between joy and overstimulation.

In aura readings, yellow appears to be the rarest of all, even more so than pure white, predominant green, or rainbow auras. Yellow's ability to absorb and become other energies likely contributes to its rarity. This absorption could explain why we see so little yellow energy, as a yellow aura might mirror or absorb the energy of another color type, effectively becoming or at least expressing and integrating that energy. A bright yellow aura is often seen as a sign of someone who is cheerful, enthusiastic, and full of energy. This person likely has a natural ability to uplift others and spread positivity. Conversely, a pale or washed-out yellow aura might indicate stress or a need for mental clarity.

Yellow light has a wavelength between 570 and 590 nanometers. This shorter wavelength and higher frequency vibrate with the energy of the Solar Plexus Chakra, which governs personal power, self-esteem, and the joy of being.

Perhaps yellow's fleeting nature adds to its unique charm, inviting us to cherish the moments of joy and optimism it brings. In this sense, the yellow type might be more fleeting, but when it appears, it lights up the aura with a vibrant, uplifting energy.

Green is the love you share with your community and the planet. It's one of the greatest healers, connecting you back to the earth. A walk in nature can do wonders for your soul, and green works the same way on the aura. Green auras are at peace because they resonate with love. If you're experiencing a difficult time, surround yourself with green by eating green foods or bringing a plant into your home.

In color psychology, green is known for its calming and balancing effects. It symbolizes growth, harmony, and freshness, often associated with safety and stability. Green has a strong emotional correspondence with tranquility and healing, making it a restful and secure color.

Davina DeSilver's *The Human Aura* explores the concept of a deeper green shade in auras. This deeper green is associated with ambition, found more prominently in business, careers, and material pursuits. DeSilver describes it as a love of growth, enjoying life, and embracing abundance. Similarly, in her book *Radiant Human*, Christina Lonsdale discusses green as a color of ambition. This deeper green connects to careers, material possessions, and wealth, reflecting a more worldly kind of love, perhaps connected to our lifestyles.

In contrast, brighter greens might represent a higher vibration of the same energy. These colors might be less attached to the material world and more focused on the zest of life and experiences. They might hold less interest in sensual pleasures and the material aspects of life in general. This is another way of understanding the power of green: a spectrum of ambition with varying degrees of worldly attachment.

Green light has a wavelength between 495 and 570 nanometers, sitting in the middle of the visible spectrum. This balanced position corresponds with the Heart Chakra, which governs love, compassion, and emotional balance. Green's central location in the spectrum reflects its harmonizing qualities, balancing the energies of the lower and upper chakras.

Green's ability to harmonize and heal makes it a powerful presence in the aura, whether it's the peaceful love of bright green or the ambitious drive of deeper green. Embracing the energy of green helps us connect to the earth and our community, fostering growth and healing in all aspects of our lives.

On the spectrum of visible light, blue is the color between violet, which represents brain energy, and green, which represents heart energy. Associated with the Throat Chakra, blue ties together the power of mind and heart through communication and self-expression. No matter how psychic you might be, you still need to communicate your inner state through your Throat Chakra.

Blue is the color of water, and water always travels the path of least resistance. Therefore, blue serves as a reminder to go with the flow. Water appears blue primarily due to the way it absorbs and scatters light. Water molecules absorb light in the red part of the spectrum and reflect light in the blue wavelengths. This effect becomes noticeable when looking at large bodies of water, like oceans or lakes, where the scattering of shorter blue wavelengths dominates. In smaller amounts, water often appears clear because the absorption of light isn't as pronounced. The blue color becomes more apparent with greater depth and volume, enhancing the scattering effect. Perhaps it is no coincidence that water absorbs red; it takes in the stress and heat of existence, calming you as it reflects cool blue back into your life. Water can fill any container, making it a powerful energy for expansion. Like a snail getting a new shell, blue helps ease a transition into the next version of yourself.

In color psychology, blue is known for its calming and soothing effects. It evokes feelings of tranquility, trust, and security. Blue can slow the pulse rate, lower blood pressure, and reduce feelings of anxiety. It encourages clarity of thought and open communication, making it an essential color for expressing one's truth.

In aura readings, a bright blue aura is often seen as a sign of a person who is calm, collected, and articulate. This person likely has a strong sense of self and is comfortable expressing their thoughts and emotions. A bright blue aura indicates someone who is honest and has a clear, confident communication style. Conversely, a dull or muted blue aura might suggest a blockage in the Throat Chakra, indicating difficulties in expressing oneself or communicating effectively.

Blue light has a wavelength between 450 and 495 nanometers. This shorter wavelength and higher frequency resonate with the Throat Chakra, which governs communication, expression, and truth. Blue's position in the spectrum reflects its bridging role, connecting the higher energies of the mind with the grounding energies of the heart.

Blue's association with water highlights its flexible and adaptive nature. Water's ability to flow effortlessly and fill any space mirrors blue's role in helping us adapt and transition smoothly. Embracing blue can encourage us to go with the flow, easing transitions and helping us expand into new versions of ourselves.

Understanding and incorporating blue's energy can enhance our ability to communicate and express ourselves authentically. By integrating blue into our lives—through visualization, wearing blue, or surrounding ourselves with blue objects—we can foster a deeper connection with our inner truth and improve our interactions with the world around us.

VIOLET

Violet and purple are distinct in their origins. Violet is a spectral color, a pure light wave at the far end of the visible spectrum. It is the natural hue our eyes perceive from the highest energy light. Purple, however, is created in the mind, a blend of red and blue light. It doesn't exist on the spectrum as its own wavelength, but instead, our brain interprets it as a mix of opposites, bridging warmth and coolness in a single, imagined hue. Because of their similarity, we will use these terms somewhat interchangeably throughout the book.

Purple represents the "eyes in the back of the head" kind of energy—the knowing before you know. Have you ever had a skill you picked up easily? That shows purple at work. Connected to the unknown and supernatural, purple allows you to connect to your clairaudience (hearing), clairvoyance (seeing), clairsentience (feeling), and claircognizance (knowing).

In color psychology, purple is associated with wisdom, mystery, and spirituality. It combines the calm stability of blue and the fierce energy of red, creating a color that evokes a sense of deep understanding and inner peace. Purple stimulates the imagination and inspires high ideals, making it a color often linked to creativity and enlightenment.

In aura readings, a vibrant purple aura is often interpreted as a sign of a person with strong intuitive abilities and a deep connection to their inner wisdom. This person is likely attuned to the spiritual realms and has a natural gift for understanding and perceiving things beyond the physical world. This is an interesting notion when considering the color "purple" does not exist except in the brain or "unseen realm." A bright purple aura indicates a high level of spiritual awareness and psychic abilities. Conversely, a muddied or dark purple aura might suggest confusion or a blockage in one's spiritual connection, indicating a need for clarity and reconnection.

Violet light is at the higher end of the visible spectrum, with wavelengths between 380 and 450 nanometers. This shorter wavelength and higher frequency resonate with the Third Eye and Crown Chakras, which govern intuition, spiritual insight, and connection to higher consciousness. Violet's position in the spectrum reflects its role in bridging the physical and spiritual worlds.

Purple's association with the supernatural highlights its ability to connect us to our higher senses. By embracing purple, we can enhance our psychic abilities and deepen our understanding of the unseen energies around us. Whether through visualization, wearing purple, or surrounding ourselves with purple objects, integrating this color into our lives can help us tap into our intuitive gifts and expand our spiritual awareness.

Understanding and incorporating purple's energy can open us to new levels of perception and insight. By working with purple, we can develop our clairaudience, clairvoyance, clairsentience, and claircognizance, gaining a deeper connection to our inner knowing and the mysteries of the universe.

Pink is the juicy love you give yourself. Whereas green is the love you share with others, pink is all about self-love. Many major religions embrace the concept of knowing thyself. Pink is a powerful color for beginning to understand the nuances of being you, by showing appreciation for all aspects of the self.

In color psychology, pink is often associated with softness, nurturing, and unconditional love. It evokes feelings of comfort, calmness, and compassion, making it a gentle yet powerful force for emotional healing. Pink encourages a nurturing attitude toward oneself, promoting self-care and self-acceptance.

In aura readings, a pink aura signifies a person who is in touch with their inner self, who values and practices self-love. This person likely has a deep understanding of their own needs and desires and takes the time to honor them. A bright pink aura can indicate someone who is kind-hearted, empathetic, and compassionate, especially toward themselves. Conversely, a pale or weak pink aura might suggest a need to focus more on self-love and personal acceptance.

Pink is not a single wavelength of light but rather a combination of red and white light. This blending of energies reflects its nature as a bridge between the grounding, passionate energy of red and the pure, enlightening energy of white. Pink's vibration resonates with the Higher Heart, or Thymus Chakra, which is often associated with unconditional love and self-compassion.

Pink's role in self-love is crucial for personal growth and emotional health. Embracing pink helps you appreciate yourself fully, acknowledging your strengths and accepting your flaws. By integrating pink into your life—whether through visualization, wearing pink, or surrounding yourself with pink objects—you can foster a deeper connection with yourself.

Understanding and incorporating pink's energy can be a transformative experience, leading to a greater sense of self-worth and inner peace. This journey of self-love is fundamental to overall well-being, providing a solid foundation for all other relationships and endeavors.

WHITE

White is the lightning strike, a moment perfectly illuminated before returning to darkness. It allows you to see things for how they are and to separate yourself from the tangle of human emotions. Associated with meditation, white provides a bird's-eye view of any situation. While red is the beginning of the journey, white marks the end. Self-actualization occurs in the energy of the Crown Chakra.

In color psychology, white is often associated with purity, clarity, and new beginnings. It symbolizes peace and serenity, and creates a sense of calm and balance. White's presence can clear the mind and open a space for fresh perspectives and insights. It is also associated with cleanliness and simplicity, often evoking a feeling of renewal.

In aura readings, a bright white aura is often seen as a sign of a person who has achieved a high level of spiritual awareness and enlightenment. This person is likely in touch with their Higher Self and possesses a deep sense of inner peace and clarity. A vibrant white aura indicates a strong connection to the divine and a clear, focused mind. Conversely, a pale or murky white aura might suggest confusion or a need for spiritual cleansing and renewal.

White light is composed of all the visible wavelengths, combining the entire spectrum of colors. This blend of wavelengths resonates with the Crown Chakra, which governs spiritual connection, enlightenment, and self-actualization. White's comprehensive nature reflects its role in integrating all aspects of the self, bringing together the physical, emotional, mental, and spiritual.

White's association with the Crown Chakra highlights its role in transcending the material world and connecting with higher consciousness. By embracing white, we can gain a broader perspective on our lives and the situations we face, allowing us to rise above emotional entanglements and see things with greater clarity. Whether through visualization, wearing white, or surrounding ourselves with white objects, integrating this color into our lives can help us achieve a state of inner peace and spiritual insight.

Understanding and incorporating white's energy can lead to profound realizations and a sense of completeness. By working with white, we can cultivate a space for meditation and self-reflection, ultimately reaching a state of self-actualization and spiritual fulfillment.

BROWN

Brown is the dirt beneath our feet. Like red, it is a very grounding color. Standing barefoot in the dirt, even for only fifteen minutes a day, has the documented effect of helping heal the body. Brown's grounding nature connects us to the earth, stabilizing and nurturing our physical form.

In color psychology, brown is associated with stability, reliability, and resilience. It evokes a sense of security and warmth, providing a solid foundation for growth. Brown's earthy tones can create a comforting environment, helping to reduce stress and promote a sense of well-being.

In aura readings, brown can sometimes be interpreted as confusion and indecision. This is because brown is a mixture of several colors, which can create uncertainty and a lack of clarity at times. A bright brown aura might indicate a person who is practical and dependable, with strong ties to the physical world. Conversely, a muddied or dark brown aura might suggest that the individual is struggling with indecision or feeling overwhelmed by conflicting energies.

Brown is not a pure spectrum color but a composite of various wavelengths. This mixture reflects its grounding qualities, as it incorporates elements of multiple colors to create a stable, earthy presence. Brown's energy resonates with the lower chakras, particularly the Root Chakra, which governs our basic needs and sense of security.

Brown's grounding influence helps anchor us in the present moment, providing a stable base from which to navigate life's challenges. By embracing brown, we can enhance our connection to the earth and foster a sense of stability and resilience. Whether through visualization, wearing brown, or surrounding ourselves with brown objects, integrating this color into our lives can help us feel more grounded and secure.

Understanding and incorporating brown's energy can also reveal areas of confusion or indecision, offering an opportunity to address and resolve these issues. By working with brown, we can achieve a balanced state of being, grounded in the earth while maintaining clarity and purpose.

BLACK

Black is a compressed rainbow that encompasses all colors at maximum density and saturation. It is a powerful color to encounter when getting to know yourself. Associated with hibernation, a black aura marks a time to step back and reevaluate your life. Black represents the night and reminds you to rest. Choosing to work with black and willingly stepping into the cave can be transformative. However, if you don't accept the need for rest, the body sometimes will take it for you, allowing the shadow aspects of black to surface.

In the psychology of color, black is often associated with mystery, power, and introspection. It symbolizes the unknown and can evoke a sense of potential and possibility. Black provides a blank canvas, encouraging deep reflection and the exploration of inner truths. However, it can also represent heaviness or depression if not approached with balance.

In aura readings, a black aura can indicate a period of introspection and self-discovery. This is a time for withdrawing from external distractions to focus on inner growth and understanding. A black aura may suggest that the person is embracing this period of self-reflection and transformation. Conversely, it may indicate unresolved fears or a reluctance to confront inner shadows. Although many people perceive a black aura as negative, associating it with darkness, death, or absence, this belief is rooted in an instinctual bias that views black as a foreboding unknown. Black, however, symbolizes much more: it is introspective and powerful, representing hibernation, rest, and renewal. While black absorbs all visible light, it also holds space for potential and growth. Instead of seeing black as an absence, it can be understood as a necessary retreat, a time for self-reflection and transformation, and the opportunity to confront and integrate our shadow aspects.

From a physics standpoint, black is the absence of visible light, absorbing all wavelengths without reflecting any. This quality of absorption reflects black's ability to encompass all experiences and emotions, providing a space for rest and renewal. Black's energy resonates with the concept of the void, a place where new potentials are born from stillness and quiet.

Black's association with hibernation highlights its role in encouraging rest and recuperation. By embracing black, we can honor the need for pauses in our lives, allowing time for reflection and healing. Whether through visualization, wearing black, or surrounding ourselves with black objects, integrating this color (or lack thereof) into our lives can help us navigate periods of transition and introspection.

Understanding and incorporating black's energy can be a powerful tool for personal growth. By willingly stepping into the metaphorical cave, we can confront our inner shadows, find rest, and emerge renewed and ready to engage with the world again.

Guided Aura Meditation

Having delved into the aura layers, chakras, and colors, we now stand at the threshold of a deeper understanding. Each layer, each hue, each energy center is a thread in the vast, luminous oniony egg of our being. To truly grasp the essence of our auras, we must weave these threads together.

The following exercise will not only enhance our perception of the aura but also deepen our connection to the subtle energies that dance around and within us. By integrating our knowledge of the layers, chakras, and colors, we open ourselves to a more profound and holistic understanding of our own energetic landscape.

Through this practice, we will uncover the dynamic relationship between our physical, emotional, and spiritual selves, embracing the full spectrum of our existence with curiosity, reverence, and wonder.

Exploring the Layers of the Aura

This exercise is designed to help you connect with your energetic body and explore the different layers that make up your aura. Before we begin, find a comfortable and quiet space where you can relax and focus without interruption. (Audio recordings of each exercise in this book are available on our website, auraweaver.com.)

1. Ground and center.
- Sit or stand with your feet firmly on the ground.
- Close your eyes and take three deep breaths, inhaling through the nose and exhaling through the mouth.
- With each exhale, visualize releasing any tension or stress.

2. Connect with the Etheric Layer.
- Hold your hands near your shoulders, as if you're holding a large ball.
- Focus on the Etheric Layer, closest to your body, about two to four inches away.
- Imagine the color red glowing in the palms of your hands.

- Feel the energy of this layer, associated with your Root Chakra, grounding you to the earth.

3. **Move to the Emotional Layer.**
    - Gently push your hands a few inches forward.
    - Visualize the color orange, representing the Emotional Layer connected to the Sacral Chakra.
    - Acknowledge any sensations or emotions that arise.

4. **Explore the Mental Layer.**
    - Push your hands out slightly further, about three to eight inches from your body.
    - Imagine a bright yellow color, symbolizing the Mental Layer associated with the Solar Plexus Chakra.
    - Reflect on your thoughts and mental processes, observing them without judgment.

5. **Experience the Astral Layer.**
    - Move your hands about a foot away from your body.
    - Envision a vibrant green color, the bridge from the physical to the spiritual.
    - Feel your heart space expanding, connecting you with the Astral Layer.

6. **Discover the Etheric Template.**
    - Extend your hands about two feet from your body.
    - Picture a deep, serene blue, representing the Etheric Template associated with the Throat Chakra.
    - Contemplate your communication and self-expression.

7. Sense the celestial body.
- Push your hands further out, approximately two and a half feet in each direction.
- Visualize a royal purple, connecting you with your Higher Self and spiritual guidance.

8. Connect with the Spiritual Layer.
- Extend your arms three feet from your body.
- Imagine a bright white light, symbolizing the Crown Chakra and the spiritual protector of your aura.

9. Explore and release.
- Move your arms in different directions, sensing the changes in the aura.
- If you encounter resistance or discomfort, imagine gently surrounding it with white light and releasing it.

10. Close the exercise.
- Slowly return your hands to your heart.
- Take a deep breath in, absorbing the energy and insights you've gained.
- Gently open your eyes and return to your surroundings, feeling more connected with your energetic self.

Remember, this exercise is a way to deepen your understanding of your energetic state. Each layer of the aura offers unique insights into our physical, emotional, mental, and spiritual well-being. Regular practice can enhance your intuition and self-awareness.

CHAPTER 2

Developing Cosmic Sight: How to See an Aura

There are two primary ways to view and interpret an aura. The first, and the one that profoundly shaped our lives and launched our business, is aura photography. We'll explore the fascinating history of aura photography in the next chapter. However, the second method of accessing the aura is a gift accessible to everyone—it requires no special equipment, only the power of your own intuition. Through developing your cosmic sight, you can sense and see the vibrant energies that surround us. In this chapter, we'll explore how to harness all of our senses to perceive the delicate dance of the aura, sharing insights and practices we've gathered along our journey.

How to Perceive the Aura

The ability to perceive auras is a deeply personal and varied experience, often influenced by an individual's unique psychic sensitivities. These sensitivities are commonly called "clair" abilities, with each representing a distinct mode of extrasensory perception. Understanding these abilities can illuminate the diverse ways people experience and interpret auras.

Recognizing that aura perception is not confined to visual experiences is essential. Sensations, feelings, sounds, and intuitive knowledge all contribute to understanding the energy fields around us. It's important for those exploring their aura perception abilities to remain open to various forms of experience, whether through seeing colors, feeling emotions, or receiving intuitive messages. Trusting in one's unique experience and understanding that aura perception, like any psychic skill, can be honed and refined over time through practice and exploration is key to developing this ability.

Below are three exercises that have helped many learn to perceive their aura. We recommend practicing these in order—from perceiving the aura of the self, then the aura of others, and finishing with the aura of the natural world. Although you may not achieve complete proficiency from doing only these exercises, they will give you a solid foundation for developing your abilities.

"CLAIR" ABILITIES

CLAIRVOYANCE, or clear seeing, enables some individuals to see auras as colors or lights surrounding a person or object. They might discern layers, patterns, or a spectrum of colors, with each symbolizing different emotional, spiritual, or physical states.

CLAIRSENTIENCE, or clear feeling, on the other hand, allows for the "feeling" of auras. People with this ability may experience physical sensations like warmth or tingling that indicate the state of someone's aura, or they might sense emotional or energetic shifts in their environment.

CLAIRAUDIENCE, or clear hearing, involves hearing sounds or voices beyond the physical realm. Those with clairaudient abilities might "hear" the energy of an aura, perceiving subtle frequencies or tones, or even words and messages when tuning into someone's energy field.

CLAIRCOGNIZANCE, or clear knowing, is the ability to intuitively know something without understanding how or why. In aura perception, this manifests as an instant understanding or insights about a person's emotional or physical well-being without relying on visual or sensory cues.

RETROCOGNITION, the psychic ability to see past events, although not directly related to seeing auras, can provide context or understanding of historical influences affecting a person's aura. For instance, past traumas or experiences may shape an individual's current aura, and someone with retrocognitive abilities may perceive and understand these influences.

Hand Aura Perception Exercise

This exercise is designed to develop your ability to perceive the subtle energy field, or aura, around your hand. By practicing this regularly, you can enhance your sensitivity to auras and energy fields. Let's begin.

1. Prepare yourself by finding the right environment.
- Find a quiet space where you won't be disturbed. Ensure there's a plain, white wall or a large white sheet of paper you can use as a background.
- Sit or stand comfortably, facing the white background.

2. Relax and focus.
- Start with a few deep breaths to relax your body and mind. Breathe in through the nose and out through the mouth, letting go of any tension.
- Rub your hands together briskly for about thirty seconds to activate the energy in your palms.

3. Position your hand.
- Hold one of your hands against the white background. Keep it at a comfortable distance from your face, usually about an arm's length away.
- Spread your fingers slightly apart and keep your hand relaxed.

4. Soften your gaze.
- Focus your eyes on the fingertips of your hand.
- Allow your gaze to soften so that you are not staring intently, but rather gazing gently. This can help in perceiving subtle energy.

5. Observe the aura.
- Continue to gaze at your fingertips and the area around your hand. Notice any changes in the air around your hand.
- You might begin to see a faint outline or a color around your hand. This could appear as a subtle light, a mist, or a color field.
- If you don't see anything initially, don't be discouraged. Aura perception can take time and practice.

6. Deepen the practice.
- Experiment with moving your hand slightly and observe any changes in the energy field.
- Try focusing on different parts of your hand—the palm, the back of the hand, each finger—and notice any differences in the aura.

7. Record your observations.
- After some time observing, lower your hand and relax your eyes.
- If you have a journal, record anything that arose during the practice, such as colors, sensations, and any emotions or thoughts you experienced.

8. Reflect and repeat.
- Reflect on the experience. How did it feel to focus on your hand's aura? What did you notice?
- Repeat this exercise regularly. Over time, you may notice an increased sensitivity and clarity in perceiving auras.

Seeing auras is a skill that develops differently for each person. Some might see colors immediately, and others may first notice a sensation or simply a clearer sense of the energy surrounding them. The key is consistent practice and openness to the experience.

Person Aura Perception Exercise

This experience aims to develop your ability to perceive the aura around another person. It can be practiced with a willing participant who can remain still for a few minutes. This practice helps with enhancing sensitivity to auras and understanding the subtle energy fields around individuals.

1. **Prepare yourself and your environment.**
   - Choose a quiet, well-lit room where you and the participant won't be disturbed. A plain, light-colored background behind the other person is ideal.
   - You and your participant should be comfortable, either sitting or standing.

2. **Relax and connect.**
   - Begin with a few deep breaths together to create a relaxed atmosphere. This helps both you and the participant to ease into a calm state.
   - If you both are comfortable, establish brief eye contact as a way to connect.

3. **Focus on the person.**
   - Ask the participant to stand or sit still. If direct eye contact is overwhelming or uncomfortable, you can focus on the space around their ear or the top of their head.
   - Gently fix your gaze on the chosen point. You should be far enough away to see the outline of their entire body but close enough to observe subtle details.

4. **Soften your gaze.**
   - Like the hand exercise, let your gaze become soft and relaxed. Avoid staring intensely; instead, maintain a gentle, diffuse focus.
   - Blink naturally and relax your eyes. This method reduces eye strain and helps with seeing auras more clearly.

5. Observe the aura.
- As you continue to gaze, observe the space around the participant's body. Look for any subtle light, color, or energy field that seems to emanate from them.
- The aura might appear as a thin, luminous film or a color cloud around the body. Note any changes in color, intensity, or texture.

6. Shift your focus if needed.
- If you find it difficult to see anything initially, shift your focus slightly. Look at different parts of their body, such as the shoulders, crown of head, or hands.
- Some people perceive energy more in terms of sensations or feelings rather than visual cues. Notice any changes in your perception as you observe.

7. Record and share.
- After the exercise, lower your gaze and allow your participant to relax.
- Share experiences with each other. If you noticed any colors or sensations, discuss them and check if they resonate with the participant's current state or feelings.

- Record your observations in a journal, noting details like color, intensity, and any intuitive insights you received.

8. Reflect and practice.
- Reflect on the experience personally and, if possible, with your participant. Discuss what felt significant or surprising.
- Practice this exercise regularly with different people to enhance your sensitivity and understanding of auras.

Remember, perceiving auras is subjective and varies from person to person. It's important to approach this exercise with an open mind and without expectations. With practice, your ability to perceive and interpret auras will grow, offering deeper insights into the energy fields of those around you.

Flower Gazing

This exercise is a meditative practice designed to enhance your ability to perceive and interact with auras. This activity can be particularly enriching for those interested in deepening their spiritual awareness and connection to nature. Let's begin.

1. **Prepare yourself and gather your materials.**
   - Choose a natural object such as a leaf, a small houseplant, or a flower. For this exercise, let's assume you have selected a flower.
   - Find a quiet, comfortable space where you can focus uninterrupted.
   - Place the flower in front of a plain, white background like a sheet of paper or a wall. This helps to reduce visual distractions.

2. **Ground and center.**
   - Sit comfortably in front of the flower.
   - Take a few deep breaths to center yourself. Inhale through the nose and exhale through the mouth, allowing your body to relax with each breath.

3. **Engage with the flower.**
   - Start by looking directly at the center of the flower. Observe its details: the colors, textures, and patterns.
   - Notice any pollen, the shape of the petals, and the way the leaves are arranged. Allow yourself to become truly curious about every aspect of the flower.

4. **Deepen your gaze.**
   - Gently shift your focus to the edge of a single petal.
   - Allow your eyes to softly unfocus and then refocus, keeping your attention on that edge.
   - Be patient and maintain a gentle, steady gaze.

5. Perceive the aura.
- As you continue to gaze, begin to notice any sensations or shifts in perception.
- You might start to see colors or feel certain emotions. Observe these without judgment.
- Stay in this state of open awareness for as long as it feels comfortable.

6. Expand your awareness.
- Slowly expand your focus from the edge of the petal to the entire flower.
- Observe any changes in the colors or feelings that may arise.
- Remember, the experience can be subtle and may not always be visual. Pay attention to all your senses.

7. Reflect and journal.
- When you feel ready, gently end the exercise with a deep breath.
- If you have a journal, take a moment to write down anything you observed, felt, or experienced during the flower gazing.
- Reflect on these observations and how they may connect to your inner state or the energy of the flower.

8. Close the practice.
- Acknowledge the time you've spent in this mindful practice.
- Thank yourself for opening up to a new experience and for any insights gained.

This exercise is not only about seeing auras but also about enhancing your mindfulness and deepening your connection with the natural world. With regular practice, you may find your ability to perceive subtle energies becomes more refined. Remember, the experience is unique to each individual, and there's no right or wrong way to perceive an aura.

CHAPTER 3

A Brief History of Aura Photography

Charlie here! My first aura photo was taken at a shop called Magic Jewelry in New York City's Chinatown. Judah and I entered a small shop packed with crystals and boxes of laminated signs explaining aura photography. An elderly woman guided us to a room at the back of the store filled with crystals. I followed her instructions, placing my hands on two metallic hand plates atop blue metallic boxes that seemed straight out of a science experiment. Inside the boxes, I learned, was a camera. Before the woman took the shot, she said, "Hold still." The shot only took seconds, but the camera's lights were blinding.

Judah was up next. After his turn, the woman pulled apart my photo on what I later learned was discontinued Fujifilm Fp-100c. A cascade of yellow developed as I looked at the image. Yellow represents joy and optimism, which I found interesting because, at that time, I was anything but. Still, yellow is an energy I seek to cultivate. The reader glanced at my aura and quickly rattled off something about how I probably needed more sleep (no surprise there). But when she got to Judah's aura—bright pink and glowing—she practically melted, holding his hand and diving into a detailed, loving analysis of every little detail. Meanwhile, I was sitting there thinking, *Do I just not have the right vibe?* and quietly wondering if I should be worried about all this aura-flirting happening right in front of me.

This experience electrified me so much that I wanted to learn how to share it with others. Through aura photography and energy work, I have come to appreciate the interconnectedness of all things, which is not only a philosophical concept but also a tangible reality that can be seen, felt, and experienced. Little did I know that this experience would lead me to cocreating over thirty thousand aura photos with so many incredible people across the world.

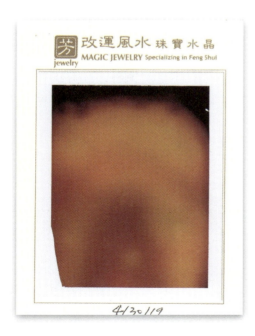
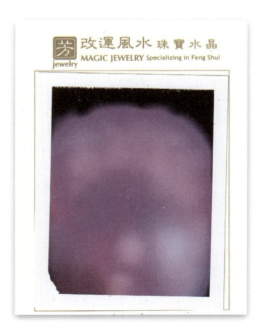

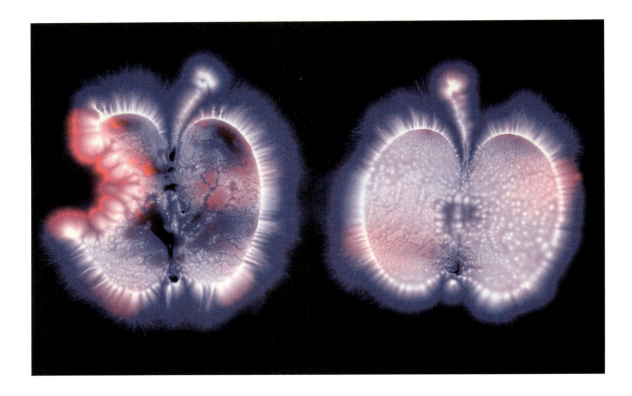

Kirlian Photography

Aura photography has its roots in the work of Kirlian photography, a system developed in 1939 by Russian electrical engineer Semyon Kirlian and his wife, Valentina. It involved a direct electrical charge to the person sitting for the photo.

The Kirlians' experiments were a wild ride. Their famous image of a leaf is a simple yet profound demonstration of the invisible life force. First, an entire leaf was photographed. Then they tore off part of the leaf and photographed it again. What they found was amazing: although part of the leaf was gone, its aura remained intact—the energetic imprint defying physical alteration. They recognized that the basis for this was just the remainder of moisture on the exposure plate, but the Kirlians had uncovered a poetic glimpse into the interconnectedness of life and energy.

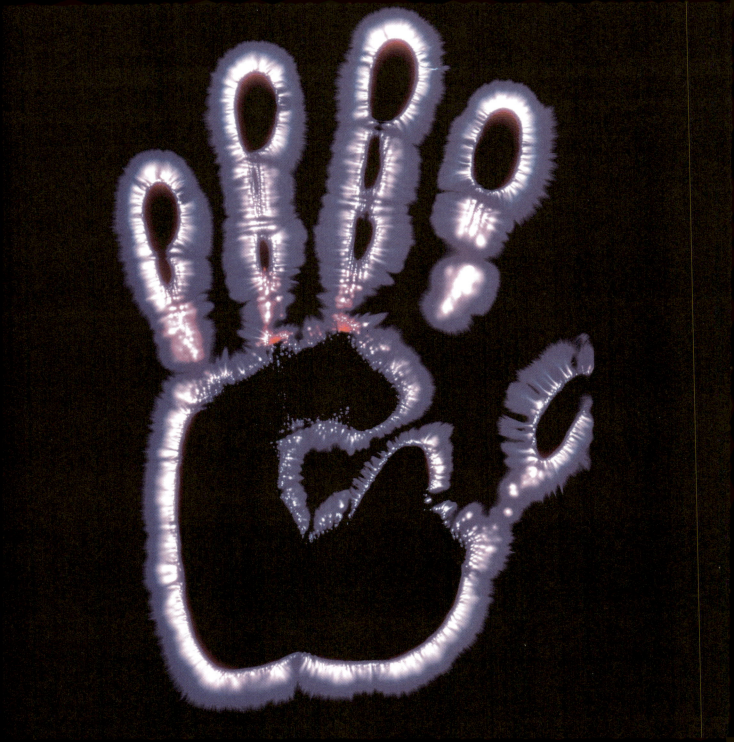

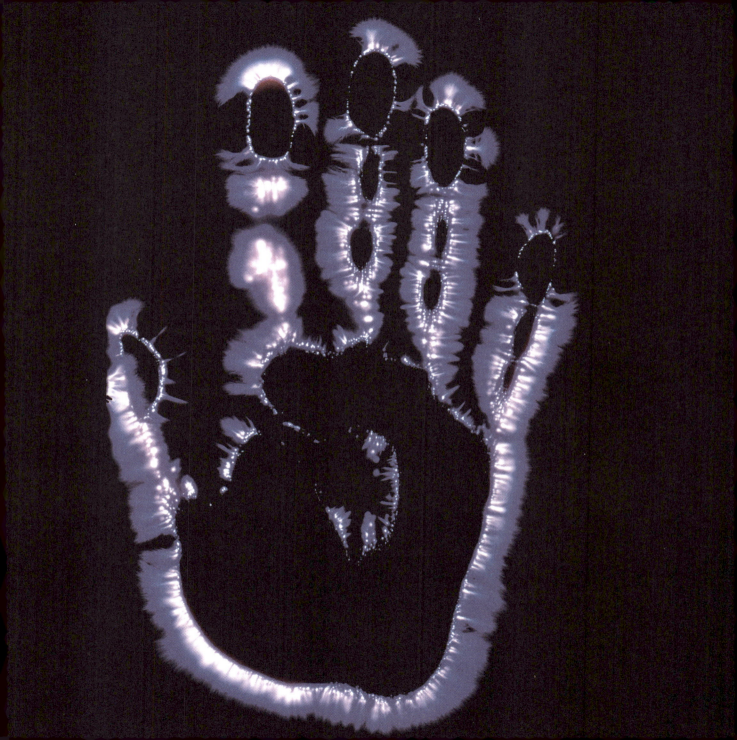

Their work extended beyond mere observation to diagnostics. For example, they used aura photographs to identify illnesses. Although this practice was controversial and one we do not endorse, it did open a dialogue about the interplay between energy and physical health. Kirlian photography became a tool for exploring deeper spiritual concepts, probing questions about the nature of our existence and unseen forces that shape our lives.

At the same time the Kirlian photography system was developed, another group, led by Samuel Hoffman and George de la Warr, was also experimenting with capturing the aura. Hoffman and de la Warr developed a technique called radionics in the 1930s and 1940s, which aimed to photograph and measure energy fields (sometimes considered "auras") around living organisms. Their work paralleled and overlapped with Semyon and Valentina Kirlian's photographic discoveries but focused more on the connection between energy fields and health.

While Kirlian photography gained more prominence in the public sphere, this second wave of energy field experimentation contributed to the broader understanding of how energy interacts with living beings, pushing the field of energy-based healing and metaphysics forward.

Victorian Ghost Photography

Humans have long used photography as a vessel to explore the unseen, pushing the boundaries of what we understand about the world around us. This fascination with the invisible realms found a particularly intriguing expression during the Victorian era through the practice of ghost photography. The Victorians, living in an age captivated by both scientific advancement and spiritualist movements, found ghost photography an enthralling blend of both worlds.

In the late nineteenth century, as photography became more accessible, it was drawn into the era's fervent interest in spiritualism. People were eager to connect with the afterlife, driven partly by the high mortality rates and the devastation of wars, which left many longing for one last connection with departed loved ones. Enterprising photographers, such as William H. Mumler, the first to claim the ability to photograph ghosts, found a willing audience. Mumler's most famous photograph is that of Mary Todd Lincoln with the supposed ghost of her husband,

President Abraham Lincoln, standing behind her with his hands on her shoulders. This photo, like many of Mumler's works, was touted as genuine proof of spiritual presence.

The process of capturing these "ghosts" was steeped in both trickery and genuine belief. Double exposure was the most common technique used, where two or more images were superimposed to create a single photograph. This would typically involve taking a photograph of an empty scene and then photographing a living person in a translucent form, using a longer exposure to create a ghostly image. The final image, often a mix of blurred shapes and discernible human forms, was presented as a haunting spectral presence caught on camera.

Public reaction to ghost photography was mixed. While many skeptics dismissed these images as mere hoaxes exploiting the grieving and gullible, others viewed them as undeniable evidence of the supernatural. The debate reached such a fervor that ghost photography was frequently discussed in serious scientific and religious forums.

Ghost photography also played a role in broader societal contexts, reflecting the Victorian's complex relationship with death and the afterlife. It underscored an era uniquely characterized by its blend of deep mourning rituals and enthusiastic embrace of technological progress. The phenomenon illustrated a cultural moment where the longing for empirical evidence of the beyond met the profound desire for reassurance about life after death.

Today, Victorian ghost photography is viewed as an early example of how media can be used to manipulate belief systems. Yet it remains a fascinating chapter in the history of photography and the cultural history of the Victorian era, shedding light on how our ancestors grappled with the mysteries of life and death. As we continue to explore aura photography and other methods of visualizing the unseen, the stories of Victorian ghost photographers remind us of our enduring quest to understand the unknown.

Modern Biofield Imaging Technologies

Although there is no direct scientific validation of the human aura as understood in metaphysical terms, there is increasing research into how the body's natural electromagnetic field can be leveraged for heath diagnostics.

The exploration of the human biofield—measurable electromagnetic fields produced by the body—offers a scientific lens through which we can better understand the phenomenon traditionally described as the aura. Research shows that the biofield is generated by the body's electrical activities, such as heart and brain function, and can be detected through modern technology. These bioelectromagnetic emissions reflect the body's physiological processes. It is the opinion of the writers that the human biofield holds important clues about our health and emotional state.

The concept of the biofield offers a bridge between esoteric and scientific perspectives. While the aura has often been seen as a reflection of a person's energy, the biofield provides a concrete, measurable aspect of this idea. Scientific studies indicate that changes in the biofield correlate with physical and emotional disturbances, much like spiritual descriptions of how the aura changes in response to health and mental conditions.

Techniques like transcranial magnetic stimulation (TMS) and magnetic resonance imaging (MRI) offer practical examples of how the biofield is already being harnessed in medical science. Both technologies rely on the body's electromagnetic properties. MRI uses powerful magnets to create detailed images of tissues based on the response of hydrogen atoms to electromagnetic fields, while TMS uses magnetic pulses to influence brain activity. These applications demonstrate how the biofield can be measured and manipulated for both diagnostic and therapeutic purposes, further reinforcing the potential of bioelectromagnetic research to bridge traditional medical practices with the understanding of human energy fields.

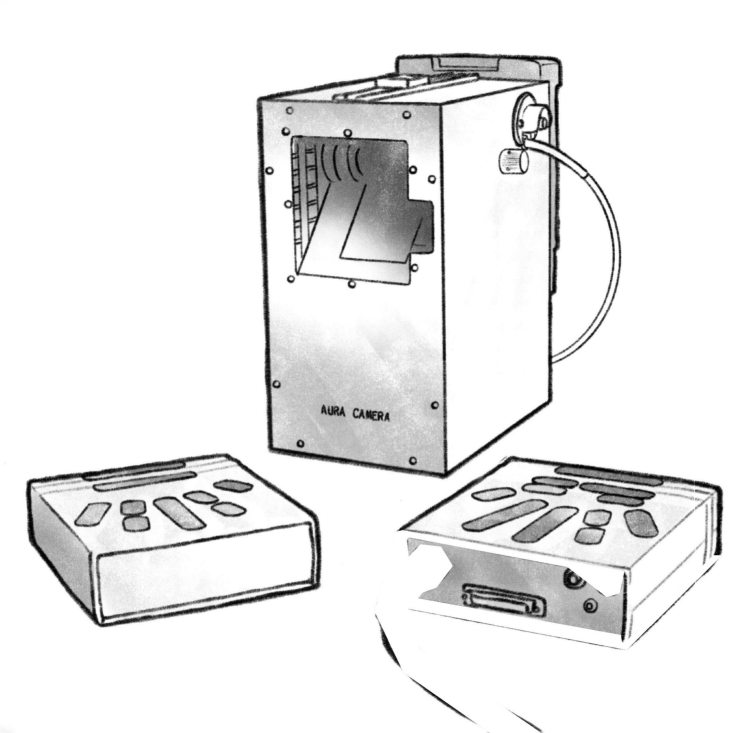

The AuraCam 6000

In the 1970s, Dr. Guy Coggins continued this exploration into seeing the unseen by developing the AuraCam 6000. He built on the legacy of the Kirlians but eliminated the need for direct electrification. Coggins collaborated with a hundred "color-seeing" psychics, harnessing the power of neural networks to create a sophisticated proprietary system for aura photography. His approach combined intuition with technology to capture the essence of the energy field.

The AuraCam 6000 avoids direct electrical charges like those used in Kirlian photography. Instead, metal hand plates channel the person's meridian channels into a camera, equipped with traditional Polaroid or modern Instax film. Surrounding the camera are banks of lights that respond to the electrical output of the individual, creating a vivid aura photograph that is as unique as a fingerprint.

How can a machine capture the ethereal, spiritual essence of our being? Consider that our organs are the physical manifestations of our spiritual centers, the chakras. Aura photography measures the tangible reflections of these energy centers, translating them into colors. Because our physical bodies nourish the aura, we can bridge the connection between these energy centers, their measurements, and the aura itself. This technology becomes a tool, revealing the intricate nature of the link between our physical form and our spiritual essence.

With this system, each photograph reveals a kaleidoscope of colors, each hue representing a different aspect of an individual's energy. The result is a snapshot of their vibrational state, a visual symphony of their unique being.

Humans have long been fascinated by the idea of seeing the unseen, and this curiosity has fueled the development of technologies like Kirlian photography, aura imaging, and even ghost photography. The drive to capture what lies beyond ordinary perception—whether the subtle energy fields surrounding living beings or the lingering presence of spirits—reflects our deep desire to connect with the invisible forces that shape our world. These attempts to photograph auras and ghosts aren't just about novelty; they represent our need to validate and explore the hidden dimensions of existence, blurring the lines between science, spirituality, and the unknown.

HOW WE FOUND DOTTIE

Charlie here again! In 2016, I was flat broke, working for a toxic company, and at a total loss for what direction my life should take. I had fled California after a string of disastrous relationships and unexplained illnesses that sent me to the hospital on and off for years. Returning home to the South, I felt defeated and exhausted. With mounting student loans and five-figure credit card debt, I turned to alcohol as my one true comfort.

I had been a social drinker, but after California, my drinking intensified. Now I drank until I blacked out. What was once a joyful, fun way to connect with my community became serious and dangerous. Today I'm very grateful to be alive.

From other mystics, I've learned that during that dark period, I was using alcohol to turn off my psychic abilities: my ability to connect with the dead, see angels out the corner of my vision, or tap into other people's energy. While this kind of extrasensory perception could be thrilling, I also felt tempted to use it in ways that felt inappropriate, and that scared me. I saw clouds of purple, blue, or gold circulate over friends when they transmuted their energy through different emotions, but I began to feel like I was spying on them.

My therapist urged me to commit to a ninety-day rehab, but I had no idea how I could afford that. Still, I had to do something, because my drinking was making me mean, even endangering my relationship with Judah, my then-boyfriend. I was overwhelmed by my work in yoga, sound healing, and meditation, all while trying to keep a wedding photography company afloat. I decided to enroll in an Alcohol Anonymous program that required attendance at ninety AA meetings in ninety days.

From an early age, I've been aware of my ability to tap into supernatural powers, even when I tried to drown it out with alcohol and sex. I have run from this power but have always returned to it. Since I was a child, I have been deeply connected to my "imaginary friends" or spirit guides. My spirituality has led me down some dark roads. I've escaped not one, but two, spiritual-based cults, thanks to deeply caring and committed friends. Despite the abuse, I always found myself leading a life filled with

ceremony, rituals, and mystic practices. Even in the depths of alcoholism, I managed to lead women's circles with the moon, read cards for those who were interested, and worked with hundreds of individuals in an energy-healing practice.

Although I had known about aura photography for years, I never considered it a viable career choice because of the cost of the camera (which, at the time, was $14,000, and is even more now). Deterred by the expense but determined to get involved in something that felt magnetic, I set out on a journey to build my own, with the help of a brilliant friend and artist, Julia Hill. But, knee-deep into designing and coding, an odd circumstance occurred: at an estate sale—for a fraction of the price—I found our flagship aura camera! We nicknamed her Dottie.

It is funny how manifestation works. On the journey to build my own aura camera, I found the original AuraCam 6000 invented by Dr. Guy Coggins himself. Little did I know then, but in the following years Dottie would allow me to photograph more than thirty thousand auras across the country.

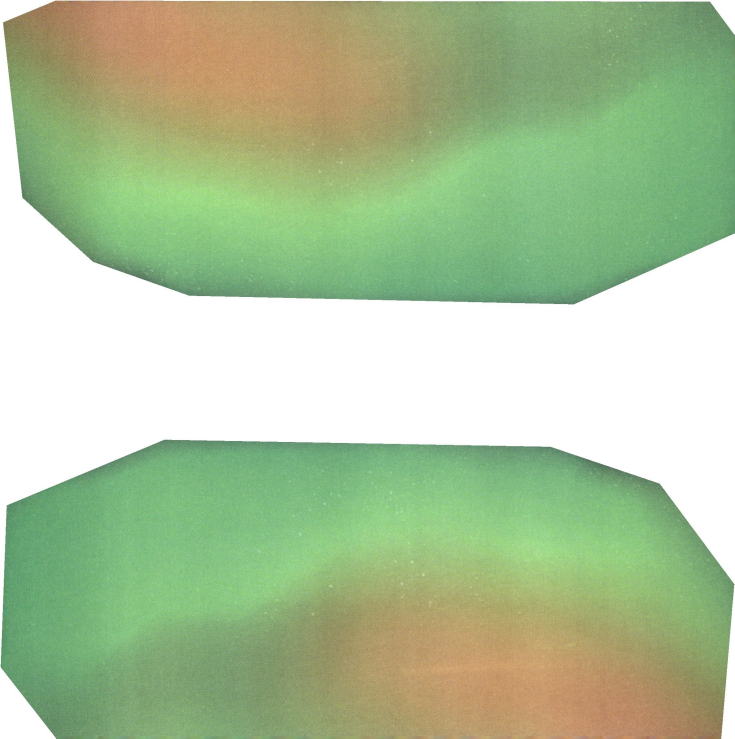

CHAPTER 4

Read the Rainbow: How to Interpret an Aura

As you learn more about how to see an aura, you will begin to realize that in the realm of the aura, colors, layers, and energy centers converge into a cohesive narrative of the self. This chapter invites you to deepen your understanding of these vibrant hues and their placements within the aura, offering a window into the intricacies between our inner worlds and the outer expressions of our being. Each position within the aura holds unique significance, revealing the complex dimensions of our experiences, emotions, and spiritual connections.

By exploring the position of the colors in the aura, we more deeply understand our external desires, internal emotions, and higher priorities. These colors and their positions are not just abstract concepts; they are reflections of our dynamic, living essence. Through this guided exploration, we aim to provide you with the tools to interpret these signals, fostering a deeper connection with your energetic field.

Positions of the Colors in Your Aura

In Chapter 1, you learned the basic features of an aura: the chakras that underlie it, the layers that comprise it, and the colors that may appear in those layers. At this point, whether using your own intuition or a printed or digital aura photograph, you can begin to analyze the composition of an aura and see how the combination and location of these features can inform the story that this dynamic energy is telling us.

1. Right Side: External Desires

The right side of the aura photo, which we believe corresponds to the right side of the person and yang energy, represents the external desires and cultivated personality of an individual. In Jungian psychology this is the Persona (more on this in Chapter 5). This is the outward face we present to the world—it acts as a social mask that shields our real self. This side of the aura can show how others perceive an individual or how they choose to present themselves publicly.

Bright, clear colors such as blue, green, or yellow typically suggest a positive, well-balanced persona. Dark or murky shades may indicate inconsistencies between how the person wants to be seen and how they actually feel or behave. A strong, consistent coloration can imply confidence and authenticity in one's public image, whereas patchy or disrupted patterns may suggest internal or social conflicts regarding one's identity or role.

2. Left Side: Internal Emotions

The left side of the aura photo, which we believe corresponds to the left side of the person and yin energy, relates to the Shadow, the private and internal Truth. This concept encompasses the parts

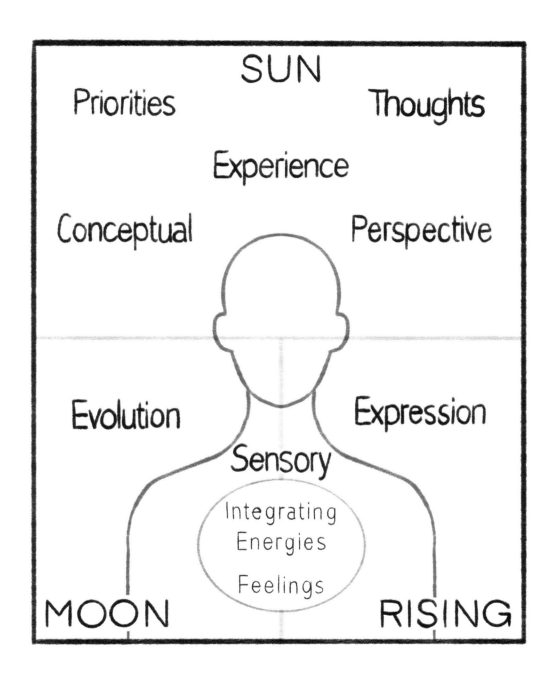

of ourselves that we sometimes deny or hide from both ourselves and the world. The Shadow contains repressed ideas, weaknesses, suppressed desires, instincts, and shortcomings.

Darker colors like reds, browns, or black can often appear in this area, possibly indicating repressed anger, unresolved pain, or hidden conflicts. Alternatively, an unexpectedly bright patch might signal an overcompensation in some area of personal struggle or a quality that the person hasn't fully integrated into their conscious personality. Viewing this side can provide clues to the traits and emotions someone may need to acknowledge and integrate to achieve personal growth and harmony.

3. Energy above the Head: High Priorities and Dreams

The area above the head in an aura photo typically reflects higher states of consciousness and spiritual aspects, or the true self.

Light, ethereal colors such as soft purples, pinks, or light blues might indicate a well-balanced relationship with *masculine* and *feminine* energies within oneself. Turbulence in this area, such as dark clouds or chaotic patterns, might suggest struggles with these energies or difficulties in relationships or self-acceptance regarding one's masculine or feminine sides. As a general note, the terms masculine and feminine aren't specific to your gender or sexuality, but are rather two complementary kinds of energy that all people have.

4. The Whole Dang Aura: The Self

The entire aura photo can be seen as representing the Self, which is the archetype that symbolizes the unification of the unconsciousness and consciousness of an individual.

A harmonious blend of colors and balanced configuration throughout the photo suggests a well-integrated Self. This indicates that the individual's internal forces are balanced and aligned, promoting a healthy psychological and spiritual state. Conversely, chaotic or fragmented patterns across the photo might indicate areas of disunity or ongoing psychological work, suggesting that the person is still in the process of integrating various aspects of the Self.

By analyzing the left and right sides of the photo along with the energy above the head, one can gain a holistic view of how a person presents themselves to the world, the traits they may be hiding, and their connection with their deeper spiritual selves. This interpretation can guide personal development and help achieve greater psychological balance and self-awareness.

Aura photography can capture more than simply colors. It often includes various phenomena such as orbs and streaks of light, which many believe to be manifestations of spiritual entities or messages. Understanding these elements can provide additional insights into an individual's spiritual guidance and connections. Here's a detailed look at what these features can signify.

Orbs in the Aura

Orbs are typically understood as spheres of light that appear in photographs. When they appear in aura photos, they are often interpreted based on their proximity to the body.

Orbs at the Top of the Aura

Orbs that appear toward the top of the aura are frequently interpreted as connections to universal spirit guides. These can include archetypal figures, deities, or even spirits that represent broader spiritual guidance and connections to the universal consciousness. The presence of these orbs can

suggest that the individual is under the protection or influence of powerful spiritual entities or forces that guide them toward their higher purpose or spiritual enlightenment.

Orbs along the top of an aura photo also relate to an individual's conscious use of their energy. This does not mean the absence of orbs indicates a person who is unconscious or without connection to spirit guides, but that the presence of orbs can mean a higher concentration of mental energy. That person can be directing willpower or experiencing a heightened state of awareness.

Orbs Close to the Body

When orbs are observed closer to the body in an aura photo, they are generally considered to represent personal spirit guides, such as ancestors or departed loved ones. These guides are thought to offer more personalized guidance, protection, and support, directly influencing the individual's personal journey and growth. Their proximity to the body suggests a close spiritual connection and an active role in the person's day-to-day life.

Orbs near the body in an aura photo represent a deep connection to the energies present. Typically we see a correlation of the orbs on the body with the orbs present along the top of the aura photo. This represents an embodied connection with higher energies, as though the individual is bringing the color into their being to physicalize or manifest the immaterial into the material.

It's important to recognize that working with spirits and ancestors is a deeply personal experience. If these interpretations do not resonate with you, the orbs may simply be manifestations of your Higher Self. Your spirituality and beliefs are uniquely your own, and these are only the frameworks we use in our practice.

Streaks of Light (Angel Lines)

Streaks of light, often referred to as *angel lines* in the context of aura photography, are believed to be direct communications from the universe or the divine. These lines are interpreted as messages from higher spiritual entities—or your Higher Self—providing guidance, affirmation, or even warnings. They are considered little nudges or pushes in the right direction, helping individuals align more closely with their spiritual paths or reminding them of the presence and support of

their spirit guides. Have you ever decided to drive home a different way and find out later you missed a wreck? This could be one of those little nudges from a spirit.

The appearance and direction of these streaks can be significant. For example, vertical lines might suggest direct downloads of spiritual energy or information, enhancing the person's intuitive capacities. Horizontal lines could indicate a need to align one's energies harmonically with universal forces.

Analyzing Orbs and Angel Lines

For individuals interested in spiritual growth or understanding their spiritual connections, analyzing orbs and streaks of light in aura photos can be enlightening. By integrating these interpretations into their spiritual practices, individuals can enhance their connection to their guides and the universal energies, fostering a more guided and spiritually aware existence.

Interpreting Colors and Patterns

Interpreting colors and patterns in an aura photo is a nuanced art that involves decoding the visual cues presented by both stable and transient energies surrounding an individual. These colors are not just random; they are reflective of an individual's emotional, spiritual, and physical state at the time of the photograph and offer deep insights into their current and enduring traits.

Although aura photography can capture us as a single dominant color at a particular time, the truth is that we hold the potential for all colors within us at all times. We may embody a particular color fully at some point, or even spend our lives primarily identified with one color. However, all the colors are always flowing and influencing us on some level.

For certain colors, the right side of an aura photo might indicate the energy a person is "calling in" or beginning to experience. For example, someone with a prominent blue area on the right might be seeking or experiencing peace and tranquility. Conversely, the left side of the photo might represent past experiences or energies a person must "give" to the world. A green aura on the left side might suggest a need to share messages of growth or a connection with nature. This could involve finding opportunities to embody and integrate these qualities.

Perhaps we can view these colors as aspects of our personality. This color system, chakra system, and aura system—along with personality typing—becomes another tool for dissecting the complexities of the self. Finding solutions to feeling stuck can involve identifying a blocked chakra and finding ways to unblock it. However, another approach exists: we can move through life embodying each color and utilizing its associated exercises. This exploration helps us discover who we truly are, navigating both smooth and challenging aspects of ourselves.

Everyday Colors

Everyday colors in the aura represent the transient and fluctuating aspects of our energy field, reflecting our immediate emotions, thoughts, and reactions to our environment. These colors, typically visible in the upper and right sides of an aura photo, can change rapidly and frequently, providing a real-time snapshot of our psychological and emotional state at any given moment. Unlike soul colors, which are deep and persistent, everyday colors are dynamic and responsive, offering insights into the nuances of our daily experiences and interactions.

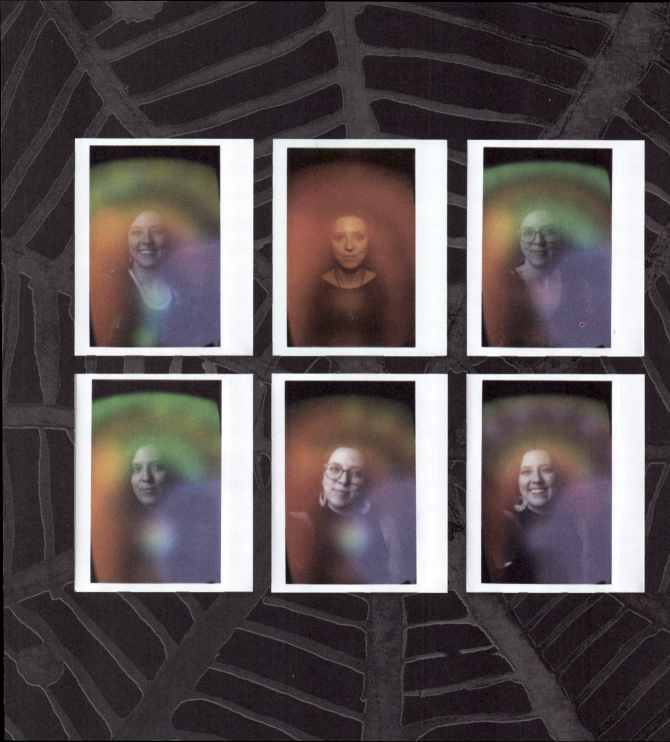

The fluid nature of everyday colors makes aura photography a valuable tool for gauging one's current emotional and mental well-being. For example, a surge of bright yellow can appear during moments of joy or intellectual engagement, indicating an active and stimulated mind. Conversely, a cloud of brown may emerge during times of stress or uncertainty, reflecting the temporary clouding of one's emotional state.

Understanding the implications of these color changes can be incredibly insightful for personal development. For instance, if someone notices a recurring pattern of red during stressful situations, it might indicate a tendency toward anger or impulsivity under pressure. Recognizing these patterns allows individuals to address and manage their responses more effectively, perhaps by adopting stress-relief techniques or exploring deeper psychological counseling to mitigate these reactions.

Moreover, everyday colors can serve as a tool that helps individuals adjust their behaviors to better align with their desired emotional states. If a person aims to cultivate grounding and tranquility but frequently sees dark purples (a color associated with being psychic and less present in the physical realm), they might consider incorporating calming activities into their routine, such as meditation, yoga, or spending time in nature, to help stabilize their aura's colors and bring them more fully into their physical form.

Additionally, the everyday colors of the aura can act as a guide for interpersonal interactions and relationships. For example, a predominance of soft pink (self-love and understanding) may suggest a period of heightened sensitivity and need for affection, guiding the individual to seek supportive social environments or communicate their needs more openly with their loved ones.

In practice, by monitoring these everyday colors, individuals can become more attuned to their internal states and learn to navigate their emotional landscapes with greater awareness and precision. This ongoing interaction with one's aura encourages a kind of energetic mindfulness, where one becomes progressively more skilled at recognizing and responding to the subtle shifts in their aura. This skill not only enhances personal growth and emotional regulation but also enriches one's understanding of how to maintain balance and harmony within themselves, regardless of external circumstances.

Ultimately, the fluidity of everyday colors in the aura presents a continuous stream of information that, when understood and utilized effectively, can lead to profound self-awareness and transformation. It empowers individuals to live more consciously and responsively, ensuring that their energies are always aligned with their highest intentions and well-being.

Soul Colors

Soul colors in the aura—those that are persistent and stable—often hold the key to understanding our deeper, more enduring traits. These colors are typically seen in areas of the aura that change less frequently and can offer insights into an individual's core strengths, challenges, and innate qualities. For example, a consistent deep blue might suggest a person who naturally embodies calmness and clarity of thought, qualities that define their approach to life's challenges. On the other hand, a vibrant and steady shade of violet might indicate a person's inherent spiritual inclinations and psychic abilities. Similar to the Big Three in astrology (Moon sign, Sun sign, and Rising sign), you are born with your soul colors, and identifying them will help you determine your life's purpose.

Interactions Between Soul and Everyday Colors

Contrasting with soul colors, everyday colors in the aura represent the more fluid and changing aspects of our lives. These colors can shift quickly and reflect our reactions to immediate situations, ongoing thoughts, and temporary emotions. For instance, a sudden flash of red in the aura may indicate a burst of passion or anger, whereas an influx of orange could suggest a recent spark of creativity or a period of social interaction. These colors help identify what energies are presently at play and what influences are affecting an individual's current state of being.

The interaction between soul colors and everyday colors can also provide insightful contrasts and comparisons. For example, if an individual's soul color is green, denoting a natural predisposition for healing and growth, but there are frequent flares of red in their everyday colors, that may suggest a conflict between their need for peace and the occurrences of stress or aggression. Recognizing these patterns can help individuals address discrepancies between their long-term traits and short-term reactions, aiding in greater self-awareness and emotional balance.

Beyond individual colors, the patterns these colors form are equally telling. For example, a clear, focused band of color at the top of the aura might suggest clear and directed thinking, whereas a muddled mix of colors around the head could indicate confusion or mental overload. Spirals of color can represent internal processing of ideas or energy, and sharp spikes may indicate a defensive or reactive energy state.

Understanding these colors and patterns not only provides insights but also practical pathways for personal development. If someone recognizes a recurrent troubling color or pattern, such as spikes of red indicating anger, they might consider strategies to manage stress or explore underlying issues causing these emotional surges. Similarly, recognizing beneficial patterns, like a consistent flow of blue and green, can affirm the practices and environments that support one's well-being, encouraging their continuation.

By delving deep into the meanings behind the colors and patterns of an aura, individuals can harness this knowledge to make informed decisions about their life and health, tailor personal growth strategies, and enhance their overall quality of life. This comprehensive approach to interpreting aura photography empowers individuals to navigate their spiritual and emotional landscapes with greater confidence and clarity.

Understanding the distinction between soul colors and everyday colors in your aura can be a profound journey into self-awareness and personal growth. While everyday colors reflect our immediate emotions and reactions, soul colors represent our deeper, more enduring traits. This exercise will guide you in identifying your soul colors and understanding their significance.

One of the simplest ways to begin this process is to ask yourself: What is my favorite color? What colors do I wear? What colors do I enjoy to eat? This can give a simple snapshot into the foundations of what your soul colors may be.

Finding Your Soul Colors in Your Aura

Discovering the difference between the shifting shades of your aura and the deeper, more constant hues of your soul colors can unlock a new level of self-awareness. Everyday colors in your aura mirror the fleeting emotions and experiences of the moment, whereas soul colors tap into the core of who you are—revealing the qualities that remain steady throughout your life. This activity is designed to help you uncover your soul colors and tap into their deeper meaning, offering insight into the true essence of your being.

1. **Prepare for aura observation.**
   - Find a quiet space where you won't be disturbed.
   - Sit comfortably and take a few deep breaths to center yourself.
   - Close your eyes and visualize a protective, calming light surrounding you.

2. **Observe your aura.**
   - If you have access to an AuraCam or similar technology, take an aura photograph.
   - If not, use a mirror in a dimly lit room with a white or neutral background. Focus on your reflection and try to perceive the subtle colors surrounding your body.

3. **Analyze everyday colors.**
   - Observe the colors that appear in the upper and right sides of your aura photo or reflection.
   - Note any bright or dominant colors, as well as any darker or murky shades.
   - Reflect on your current emotional state, thoughts, and recent experiences. How do these colors correlate with what you're feeling right now?

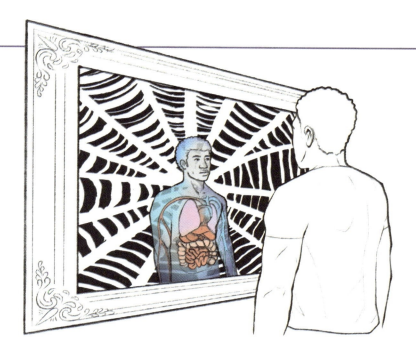

4. Identify persistent soul colors.

- Look for colors that remain consistent over time, particularly in the lower parts of the aura or areas that change less frequently.
- These stable colors often represent your core strengths, challenges, and innate qualities.
- Compare these observations with known attributes of soul colors. For example:
  - **Deep blue:** calmness, clarity of thought, introspection.
  - **Violet:** spiritual inclinations, psychic abilities.
  - **Green:** healing, growth, empathy.
- Consider how these soul colors align with your personality, behaviors, and life experiences.

5. Reflect on contrasts and interactions.
- Compare your soul colors with the everyday colors in your aura.
- Reflect on any contrasts or conflicts. For example, if your main soul color is green (healing and growth) but you see frequent flashes of red (stress or anger), consider how these energies interact.
- Think about what these patterns reveal about your inner state and how you can address any imbalances.

6. Apply practically.
- Use your insights to guide personal development. If you notice troubling colors like frequent red spikes, consider stress management techniques or deeper psychological exploration.
- Affirm beneficial patterns by continuing practices that support your well-being, such as meditation, yoga, or spending time in nature.

7. Document your journey.
- Keep a journal of your observations, reflections, and any changes you notice in your aura over time.
- Note how different activities, environments, or emotional states influence your aura.

By engaging with this exercise, you'll gain a deeper understanding of your soul colors and how they shape your interactions with the world. Embrace the dynamic interplay of everyday colors and soul colors as a tool for continuous self-discovery and growth.

CHAPTER 5

Aura Archetypes

The concept of archetypes in auras stands out as one of the most innovative and intriguing explorations into the realm of aura reading, venturing beyond traditional analysis into pioneering territory. Unlike conventional studies of personality archetypes or the color-specific attributes known in other disciplines, the notion of aura archetypes delves into the unique signatures visible in aura photography, which are seldom explored to this depth. This exploration feels like a leap into new technology, tapping into uncharted areas of aura interpretation to uncover how humanity aligns with our evolving understanding of these energies that we are co-creating with you in the present moment.

Much like the Major Arcana of tarot, participants in our aura photography experience seem to exhibit archetypal characteristics in their aura photos. Whereas the Major Arcana are aspects of the self that each person can be cyclically battling symbolically or literally, the aura archetype "system" portrays correlative qualities. We present what we have found in hopes of inspiring deeper investigations around self-discovery.

Using the template of the Major Arcana, and correlations of powerful symbols and sacred structures, including sacred geometry and esoterica, we can overlay the similar principles of the human aura and aura photography to produce this set of aura archetypes.

An aura archetype is a specific pattern or configuration of energy within an individual's aura that embodies particular personality traits, emotional states, and spiritual inclinations. These archetypes are deeply influenced by Carl Jung's psychological concept of archetypes, which he described as universal, archaic symbols and images inherent in the collective unconscious, shaping human behavior and experiences.

In the context of aura readings, these archetypes manifest as visible expressions in one's energy field. The aura acts as a dynamic mirror of an individual's internal state, displaying emotions, health, and spiritual well-being through various colors and patterns. For example, aura archetypes such as the Healer, Teacher, Warrior, or Visionary are each associated with distinct colors and shapes in the aura. A Healer may display a green aura, symbolizing growth and balance, whereas a Warrior may show strong red tones, indicating energy and passion.

Understanding our aura archetype provides valuable personal insights, revealing innate strengths and predispositions. This awareness can guide personal and spiritual growth by helping us align our life choices with our deepest potential, leading to a more purposeful existence. Additionally, in social or group settings, recognizing the different aura archetypes can improve communication and dynamics by providing deeper understanding into our inherent tendencies and needs. It is our belief we are codifying a compelling framework for exploring the intricate connections between our energetic and physical lives, enhancing personal development, therapy, and spiritual exploration.

Aura archetypes, as discussed here, offer a perspective on how auras reflect individual paths and personality traits. We explore several specific archetypes, each correlating with distinct life paths and personal characteristics, and how they are illustrated vividly through the lens of an aura photographer.

The Manifestor Aura

A striking example is the Manifestor Aura, typically marked by a robust red band topped by an overarching purple or pink band. This aura archetype is often seen in individuals embodying both Technical and Visionary roles. The dual-color representation signifies a pivotal moment where decisions and transformations converge, signaling both action and deep introspection. This archetype is particularly common among leaders who balance hands-on responsibilities with overarching strategic visions, embodying the essence of transformative decision-making.

Strengths

LEADERSHIP AND VISION: Individuals with the Manifestor Aura possess a unique blend of hands-on pragmatism and visionary foresight, making them effective leaders who can both conceive of and implement strategic visions. They aren't just the technician on the ground, they also have to be the eye in the sky.

DECISIVENESS: Robust red energy enables quick and confident decision making, especially in critical situations where clear direction is needed.

INFLUENCE AND CHARISMA: The vibrant colors of this archetype often draw others to them, making them influential figures in their personal and professional circles.

Weaknesses

OVERDOMINANCE: Their strong presence and decisive nature can sometimes be experienced as overbearing, potentially overshadowing or stifling the contributions of others.

BURNOUT: Any strong leader type, like the Manifestor Aura, tends to overmanage without delegation. Balancing intense leadership responsibilities can lead to stress and burnout if not managed properly.

RIGIDITY: Their clear vision and strong will might make them resistant to alternative ideas or adaptive changes, especially when diverging from their planned path.

The Crossroads Aura

Another compelling archetype is the Crossroads Aura. The visual of this aura is greatly similar to the Manifestor Aura. The difference is that the bold, decisive red band of the Manifestor Aura is replaced by a much more reserved red color, the texture of which has a more gentle gradient. The red-colored band across the top may be more pronounced, suggesting that the imaginative, mental qualities are more pronounced than the physical. The aura overall may seemed compressed and much closer to the body. Individuals exhibiting this aura are often at a critical juncture, making significant life-altering decisions. The aura visually captures this dynamic, with colors that suggest deep contemplation and potential change. It represents a state of gathering energy and ideas, a reservoir of potential waiting to be directed toward new ventures or life paths.

Strengths
ADAPTABILITY: Individuals with the Crossroads Aura are at a point where adaptability is crucial, and their energy has been split between the physical reservation of energy (red) and the unrealized change they are bringing from the mental world (purple) to their reality.

INTROSPECTION: They are typically very introspective, considering the time and energy spent to imagine and contemplate an imminent, life-altering choice.

POTENTIAL FOR GROWTH: This aura marks a phase of significant personal growth and transformation, giving individuals the chance to redefine their paths and align more closely with their true selves.

Weaknesses

INDECISIVENESS: Being at a crossroads can sometimes lead to paralysis by analysis, where the fear of making the wrong choice leads to indecision. The red energy near the body can take on a dense, heavy feeling for the individual. A well-rehearsed groove can easily feel like a rut where one is stuck and finding it difficult to evolve toward the dream in their mind's eye.

ANXIETY: The uncertainty of major life decisions can cause stress and anxiety, which might cloud judgment or emotional well-being. More often than not, reality won't match the perfect picture in our head; it's easy to over-worry if you are prone to perfectionism.

TRANSITIONAL VULNERABILITY: During times of change, individuals may feel more vulnerable to negative influences or doubt, affecting their confidence and clarity.

The Artist Aura

We also discuss the Artist Aura, which blends the vibrant energies necessary for dynamic creative expression with the more subdued tones that suggest steady leadership. This aura archetype is common among those who need to innovate continuously while providing stable guidance to others, such as those in creative industries who must balance their artistic instincts with business or team leadership responsibilities. The colors of this aura can vary between the warm and cool tones of the spectrum. The Artist Aura can be bright, pastel, or deep blues, relating to poets, musicians, singers, and speakers in strong resonance with their voice as a means of expression and creativity. Alternatively you may see traditional fine artists who use the medium of canvas, clay, or photography exhibiting a fiery red-orange.

Strengths
CREATIVITY AND INNOVATION: Those with this aura are natural innovators, capable of thinking outside the box and introducing new ideas and solutions.

BALANCED LEADERSHIP: They are able to balance creative impulses with practical implementation, making them effective leaders in fields that require both artistic vision and organizational skills. Our fire-orange auras have a collaborative spirit, and seek constant feedback. We notice the bluer auras are more introspective, with ample private creation time before presentation.

INSPIRATION: Their ability to materialize and speak their inner truth of their muse serves as an inspiration to others. Our blues can speak deeply to process and philosophy with intellectual insight, while our fiery oranges are ready to expand our minds by taking us on a trip of sheer willpower.

Weaknesses

CONFLICT BETWEEN CREATIVITY AND PRACTICALITY: Balancing creative desires with the realities of physical limitations can be a constant struggle. A great vision can be dashed by a premature reality check.

INCONSISTENCY: The drive for continuous innovation may lead to inconsistency in plans and expectations, potentially confusing or alienating collaborators and patrons.

OVEREXTENSION: Trying to fulfill the never-ending depth of one's creative vison is a great way to lose lots of sleep. At some point, we must learn how to say "no" to others and ourselves.

The Intuitive/Witch Aura

The Intuitive or Witch Aura, characterized by deep purples and luminous whites, is often associated with those who have a natural affinity for the metaphysical or spiritual realms. These individuals may possess heightened intuitive abilities, often expressing themselves through healing, psychic, or shamanic practices. Their aura reflects a profound connection to the ethereal, with colors that suggest a life attuned to spiritual dimensions.

Strengths

DEEP INTUITION: Individuals with this aura have highly developed intuitive abilities, allowing them to perceive and understand things beyond the ordinary.

SPIRITUAL CONNECTION: Their deep connection to spiritual or metaphysical realms provides them with unique insights and guidance, often perceived as wisdom by others.

HEALING ABILITIES: Many with this aura are natural healers, capable of understanding and manipulating energies to foster healing in themselves and others. We see our therapists and energy healers in this archetypal aura.

Weaknesses

EMOTIONAL SENSITIVITY: Their heightened sensitivity, although a strength, can also leave them vulnerable to emotional turbulence and psychic overload.

MISUNDERSTANDING FROM OTHERS: Their deep connections to the ethereal can sometimes be misunderstood by those with a more conventional outlook, leading to feelings of isolation, alienation, and sometimes suppression through substance use.

ENERGY DEPLETION: Managing intense spiritual and emotional energies can be draining, requiring them to find balance to avoid exhaustion. This is especially true for the gifted intuitive without a modality to conjure protections.

The Rainbow Unicorn Aura

On a lighter note, the Rainbow Unicorn Aura represents those whose lives are a tapestry of varied but harmonious experiences, reflecting the joy and creativity that color every aspect of their being. This aura is vibrant and multicolored, indicating versatility and an openness to life's myriad possibilities. We categorize the rainbow aura as an aura showing little to no predominant aura color, characterized by having three or more colors present in the aura.

Strengths

INSPIRATION: Rainbow Unicorn Auras are typically very bright and positive. It's rare that a very multi-colored aura would attach to a low-energy person. These unicorns radiate positivity and creativity, often uplifting those around them. They typically have a presence when entering a room.

ADAPTATION: With vast stores of energy, this aura can overcome great obstacles through sheer willpower. In work life, this person may be required to wear many hats, activating many different chakras at the same time.

CHARISMA: They inspire joy and wonder, often leading by example in embracing life's diversity. Rainbow unicorn auras with pink and purple can be very eclectic and charismatic personalities. These auras really want to make a strong first impression.

Weaknesses

INCONSISTENCY: Although versatility can be a strength, this aura can also be perceived as unpredictable. Sometimes this aura indicates someone who is spread thin across multiple pursuits. A heightened energetic state is unsustainable, and many Rainbow Unicorns may be burning the candle at both ends and on the verge of burnout.

DISTRACTIBILITY: The downside to openness. These auras have a varied zest for life, and can struggle to maintain a clear direction.

SUPERFICIALITY: Their lack of focus can sometimes prevent them from reaching the depth of understanding or mastery in any one field. They may find new ideas exciting but struggle to follow through as the novelty fades.

The Open-Hearted Aura

The Open-Hearted Aura is seen in those who lead with love and compassion, often caregivers and educators like elementary school teachers, and who consistently show up authentically for those they serve. Their aura radiates a steadfast green, symbolizing a life led with purpose and deep care for others.

Strengths

COMPASSION: People with the Open-Hearted Aura are usually very friendly. They can balance their empathy with action, meaning they are incredibly empathic without becoming the energy and they stay rooted in their being.

COMMITMENT TO PRINCIPLES: Green colors in the head of the aura can symbolize strong opinions or a deep-set point of view.

GROUNDEDNESS: A very rare type of aura, this aura has the color green in the mental and physical areas and shows the person may have a deep connection to plants, either plant lovers with many plants in the home or practitioners who use plants in their daily lives. They may also just love the outdoors and have deep reverence for nature.

Weaknesses

MARTYRDOM: A deeply empathic and overly self-sacrificing Open-Hearted Aura may have difficulty setting intentional boundaries.

CONFLICT AVOIDANCE: Shadow denying or toxic positivity can dim the light of this aura. The preference for avoiding confrontation and keeping the peace may prevent them from addressing important issues or standing up for themselves when necessary.

INSECURITY: With their empathic nature, the praise they receive from caregiving could become a dependency for self-validation. Other people have expressed being overly opinionated, ridged in their point of view, or overly self-critical.

The Peacemaker Aura

Individuals with the Peacemaker Aura typically exhibit soft, pastel shades, particularly in blues and greens, which signify tranquility and a natural ability to soothe conflicts. These auras often appear smooth and flowing, indicating a person who naturally gravitates toward mediation and harmony. Peacemakers are essential in any community or organization as they facilitate understanding and foster a peaceful environment.

Strengths
PEACEMAKING: Peacemakers don't simply avoid conflict—they address it by fostering understanding and encouraging all sides to find common ground.

EMPATHY: Peacemakers are strong empaths. They mentally and physically begin to resonate with the different emotional experiences with those around them, connecting deeply with others.

DIPLOMACY: Especially our deep blues, the Peacemaker reflects the effective communication endowment of the Throat Chakra. They speak with articulate calmness while maintaining trust around conflicting energies.

Weaknesses

PEOPLE-PLEASING: Conflict avoiders to a fault, the Peacemakers are people pleasers, which can lead to sacrificing too much of themselves to maintain the peace.

OVER-ACCOMMODATION: People-pleasing can morph into a reduction of one's voice and insight—which is the main strength of the Peacemaker's conflict resolution abilities.

BURNOUT: As an energetic diplomat, the Peacemaker is constantly alchemizing heightened emotions into tranquility. This is very draining, as the Peacemaker must experience all the emotions in order to transmute them.

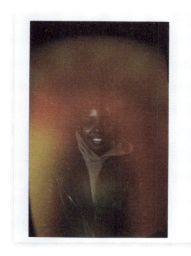  

The Explorer Aura

The Explorer Aura is characterized by vibrant orange and flashes of gold, reflecting a bold and adventurous spirit. These individuals are often on a quest for new experiences and knowledge, driven by an innate curiosity about the world. Their auras pulsate with energy, showing an enthusiasm for life that encourages them to push boundaries and explore uncharted territories, both literally and metaphorically. These auras resonate with our Artist Aura because they are kindred spirits of adventure.

Strengths

INNOVATION: Like our Artists, the Explorer does not like to be bored! Well, who does? But the Explorer would take personal offense to stifling energy.

RISK-TAKING: Uniqueness is synonymous with the bold self-expression. The Explorer is a pioneer in this regard. With a deep respect for curiosity and discovery as life's purpose, they are constantly evolving.

VERSATILITY: Their constant evolution allows them to thrive in changing environments and unfamiliar situations. They have a flexibility and ease to going with the flow of life.

Weaknesses

RESTLESSNESS: Explorers may struggle with commitment in relationships or long-term projects. The quest for novelty means they are quick to suffer boredom.

DISCONTENTEDNESS: Routine and stagnation can build character in others, whereas the Explorer may become fixated on fulfillment through tackling the next big thing, overlooking what they already have.

UNRELATABLE: Explorers may overlook important details, as details are seen as roadblocks. This separates the Explorer from fulfilling and substantive experiences that require patience and thoroughness. Their tendency to rush ahead can leave them disconnected from important aspects of their environment and the people around them.

The Visionary Aura

Those with a Visionary Aura exhibit clear, bright indigo or deep violet hues, indicating a connection to higher consciousness and a capacity for profound insight and innovation. Visionaries are the dreamers and creators who bring new ideas into reality, often acting as catalysts for societal change. Their auras suggest a depth of thought and a focus on future possibilities.

Strengths

VISION: Visionaries possess an extraordinary ability to look beyond the current moment and imagine future potentialities. They are often able to "foresee" pathways because of this tendency to imagine circumstances for potential outcomes. This may cause others around them to be confused at their forward-thinking decisions.

LEADERSHIP: The Visionary is a natural leader because their innovative thinking and insights inspire others to follow them. But don't expect a Visionary to seize monetary or political power; they are more like a spiritual leader that tends to acquire disciples.

INSIGHT: Their ability to understand complex and abstract concepts is second to none. The connection to both the Third Eye and Crown suggests they hold a strong connection to bridging the gap between the material world and the higher realms of thought.

Weaknesses

IDEALISM: While their visions are often grand and transformative, Visionaries can sometimes become overly idealistic, losing touch with practical realities. They may lose their manifestation energies through a maze of mentality and overintellectualization.

IMPRACTICALITY: At times this archetype can be so focused on the big picture and the future that they overlook the details necessary to bring their ideas to fruition. Although they excel with conceptualization, they struggle with implementation.

ABSTRACTION: The Visionary can come across as aloof or detached from everyday life. They may seem distant and have a tendency toward isolation and introversion. This can lead to challenges with being understood and connecting with others.

The Healer Aura

The Healer Aura has many color templates. They can radiate in warm, enveloping shades of pink and soft orange and white. They can embody a version of Manifestor Aura with a mix of a softer red with voluminous pink. They can also resemble the Open-Hearted Aura with a strong presence of green but a mixture of whites and blues. This aura is commonly found in those who dedicate themselves to helping others, whether through caregiving professions, parental roles, or acts of kindness in daily life. The gentle flow of their aura's energy soothes those around them, providing comfort and support.

Strengths

NURTURE: One of our readers, Raina Gars, calls a certain color combination sometimes seen in the Healer Aura "The Inner Child." This mix of white, pink, and warm orange combines the energies of clarity, creativity, and love, much like our younger selves. When this template is present, the nonjudgmental innocence of our Inner Child is compassionately guiding us.

SUPPORT: The presence of the Healer Aura is stabilizing and helps others feel seen and valued. This attentiveness is not only a form of caregiving but also a form of emotional intelligence.

DEDICATION: A strong presence of green in the Healer reflects the aspect of integrity and duty regarding relationships. Whether they are taking care of family members, clients, or friends, their aura embodies a sense of devotion, which drives them to offer their support tirelessly.

Weaknesses

SELF-DEPRECATION: As anticipated, the auras heralded for being givers tend to have a weakness of giving so much they have to burn out in order to recover. What we can all learn from this common folly is the energy alchemy of cocreation with those we wish to truly help.

OVERBEARINGNESS: Empaths, intuitives, and the Healer can become enmeshed in the life circumstances of others and take on too much emotional responsibility. They can feel responsible for fixing every problem they encounter and overstep their boundaries.

CONTROL: In a misguided desire to assist and protect, the Healer may become overprotective and controlling. They may attempt to shield others from hardship, thereby preventing agency and opportunities to learn valuable life lessons.

The Warrior Aura

Individuals with the Warrior Aura display bold, encompassing reds and few accents, and typically a great concentration of energy around the body, symbolizing strength, courage, and a readiness to face challenges head-on, with little overthinking involved. Warriors are protectors and advocates, often found on the front lines of crisis situations or leading campaigns for justice and change. Their auras exude a powerful presence that can command attention and inspire others to action.

Strengths

BRAVERY: Individuals with this aura have a fearless approach to life, confronting challenges head-on and often taking leadership roles in times of crisis. Their boldness allows them to remain calm and focused under pressure, making them invaluable in situations that require decisive action.

RESILIENCE: These individuals are driven mostly by the deep inner fire of the foundational Root Chakra, allowing them to persist through adversity and recover quickly from setbacks. Their resilience is not just physical but also mental and emotional, as they often rise above personal hardships with unwavering determination.

AUTHORITY: The presence of the Warrior Aura alone has a powerful, authoritative quality, making them natural leaders in both personal and professional realms. This is the archetype that will seize power, or step into a role if a vacuum appears.

Weaknesses

FORCEFULNESS: The intensity of the red in the Warrior Aura may lead them to take a confrontational approach, even when diplomacy or gentleness would serve them better. Their instinct to protect or fight can cause them to react too strongly, especially when they perceive a threat.

RECKLESSNESS: Warriors often act with speed and decisiveness, but this can sometimes lead to impulsive behavior.

GUARDEDNESS: Individuals with the Warrior Aura are often highly guarded, preferring to maintain a strong, impenetrable exterior. This serves them well in times of crisis, but it can also make it difficult for them to show vulnerability or ask for help when they need it. The strength of their aura may create an impression that they don't need support, even when they are struggling internally. This guardedness can isolate them from deeper emotional connections, as they may fear that showing weakness will undermine their leadership or authority. Warriors must learn that true strength sometimes lies in vulnerability and allowing others to help.

Each of these aura archetypes offers a unique set of characteristics and energies, reflecting the diverse paths and roles individuals may embody in their lifetimes. By understanding the specific energies and patterns within their auras, people can gain deeper insights into their personalities, strengths, challenges, and the dynamics of their interactions with the world. However, not all auras will fit neatly into one archetype. Some may blend multiple energies or exist beyond the scope of these categories, reflecting the complexity and fluidity of human experience.

The archetypes help to map out the complex landscape of human emotions, traits, and potential, presented through the unique visual language of auras. This chapter aims not only to introduce these archetypes but also to provide readers with tools to identify and understand their own aura signatures. Through engaging with this new dimension of aura photography, individuals can gain insights into their personal journey toward authenticity, aligning their external life with their inner truth. As we navigate through these pages, we invite readers to reflect on their own auras, exploring the profound implications these energies have on living an authentic life.

It's important to emphasize that these archetypes represent cycles, not prescriptions or predetermined paths. They are not about being permanently stuck in the "power" side, but rather about preparing for a period of rest, a denouement, a yin to the yang. The goal is to participate in the cycle, not to strive for an impossible permanent alignment with the "power" phase. Likewise, the uniqueness of each aura means that many may move fluidly between archetypes or resonate with none at all, reinforcing that there is no singular path to authenticity.

Advanced Aura Reading Using Jungian Principles

Carl Jung's psychological concepts provide a rich framework for interpreting aura photos, offering deeper insight into the psyche through the energy captured in the aura. Jung believed that the psyche consists of both conscious and unconscious elements and that archetypes are the universal patterns residing in the collective unconscious. Jung's comprehensive model includes twelve distinct archetypes, which are further grouped into categories based on soul, ego, and self types. We have adopted a truncated model and other Jungian concepts to interpret auras using the principles of Self, Persona/Ego, Shadow, Anima, and Animus—all of which play significant roles in shaping our psychological and spiritual lives.

Aura Correspondences

COLOR	CHAKRA	PLANET	DAY
RED	ROOT	MARS	TUESDAY
ORANGE	SACRAL	MERCURY	WEDNESDAY
YELLOW	SUN	SOLAR PLEXUS	SUNDAY
GREEN	HEART	VENUS	FRIDAY
PINK	HEART	VENUS	FRIDAY

MUSICAL NOTE	BODY PART/ ORGAN SYSTEM	AURA LAYER	KEY WORDS
C	SKELETON, LEGS, FEET	ETHERIC (VISCERAL)	GROUNDED, SAFETY, FIRST STEPS
D	KIDNEYS, WATER, SEX ORGANS	EMOTIONAL	CREATIVITY, MANIFESTATION
E	DIGESTION, NERVOUS SYSTEM	MENTAL	JOY, ABUNDANCE, HEALTH
F	BLOOD, HEART, BREAST	ASTRAL	UNCONDITIONAL LOVE, NATURE
F#	BLOOD, HEART, BREAST	ASTRAL	SELF-LOVE, APPRECIATION

Aura Correspondences

COLOR	CHAKRA	PLANET	DAY
BLUE	THROAT	NEPTUNE	N/A
PURPLE	THIRD EYE	JUPITER	THURSDAY
WHITE	CROWN	MOON	MONDAY
BROWN	ROOT	EARTH	N/A
BLACK	N/A	SATURN	SATURDAY

MUSICAL NOTE	BODY PART/ ORGAN SYSTEM	AURA LAYER	KEY WORDS
G	VOCAL CHORDS	ETHERIC	COMMUNICATION, EXPANSION
A, B	BRAIN	CELESTIAL	IMAGINATION, CLAIRVOYANT
N/A	BRAIN	SPIRITUAL	INTEGRATION, HUMILITY
N/A	N/A	N/A	GROUNDING, CONFUSION
N/A	N/A	N/A	HIBERNATION

APPLYING JUNGIAN PRINCIPLES

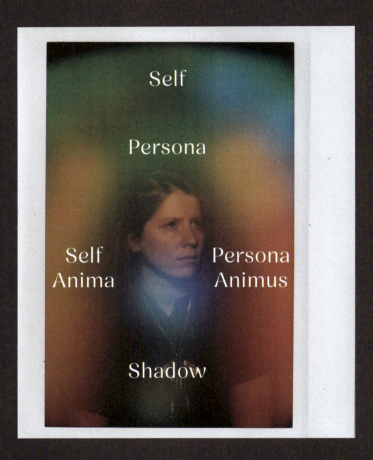

The Persona
This type represents the social face an individual presents to the world, acting as a mask that's designed to make a specific impression upon others while concealing that person's true nature. In aura photos, the colors and patterns that may correspond to the Persona can reveal how a person perceives themselves or wishes to be perceived by the external world.

The Shadow
Often seen as the darker side of the ego, the Shadow contains those parts of ourselves that we reject or do not wish to acknowledge. This includes negative impulses and hidden fears, as well as latent potential and untapped creativity. In aura readings, dark or murky areas may suggest Shadow aspects coming to the fore, prompting the need for self-reflection and integration.

The Anima/Animus
These types represent the feminine and masculine dimensions within each person, respectively. The Anima/Animus is seen as a bridge to the collective unconscious and plays a critical role in our relationships and how we connect on a deep, often unconscious level with others. In aura photos, imbalances or particular emphasis in colors may reflect the state of one's Anima or Animus, offering insights into how gender dynamics are influencing a person's current life situation.

The Self
Symbolizing the unification of the unconscious and conscious parts of the mind, the Self is the type that represents the entirety of the psyche. It is seen as the ultimate goal of personal development and psychological integration. Aura images that show a harmonious blend of colors and a balanced saturation and configuration suggest a well-integrated Self. Chaotic or fragmented patterns may indicate areas of disunity or ongoing psychological work.

How to Use Jungian Archetypes to Read Auras
With these Jungian concepts in mind, interpreters of the aura can approach their readings with a nuanced understanding of what the colors and shapes may be disclosing about a person's inner life and psychological state. For instance:

- Bright, clear areas in the aura can suggest a well-functioning Persona, where the individual is successfully balancing their inner and outer lives.
- Spots or clouds could indicate manifestations of Shadow, unresolved issues, or feelings of confusion.
- A vibrant or dominant color may reflect an active Anima or Animus influence.
- A radiant or particularly cohesive aura could suggest the presence of a strong, integrating Self.

For the motivated seeker, the full Jungian archetype model may offer more insightful context and a deeper understanding of applying the model to interpreting auras.

Reading an aura photo through the lens of Jung involves interpreting the colors and patterns visible around a person, captured by specialized photography that reveals the energy fields surrounding the human body. These photos combined with archetypes can provide deep insights into a person's emotional and energetic state. In a Jungian context, different areas of the aura photo relate to distinct aspects of the psyche: the Persona, the Shadow, and the Anima/Animus.

How We Conduct Aura Readings

When we conduct readings at Aura Weaver events, we integrate these concepts. We believe it's important to utilize this ancient system of imagery, symbology, and esoteric knowledge. Eliza Swan, in her book *The Anatomy of the Aura*, refers to *sacred synesthesia*, or the ability to use light, numbers, and images to broaden our intuitive capacities and draw deeper meaning from an aura photo. This "aura thumbprint" captures a person's essence at a specific moment.

What began as a way to pass the time while waiting for photos to develop became an integral part of the process. Regardless of whether a photo is fully developed, we find that combining the aura reading with tarot, oracle cards, archetypes, imagery, and symbology significantly deepens our understanding. These elements offer numerous correspondences that bolster our interpretations and create a stronger connection with the client. The refined system of symbology, numerology, and archetypes within tarot and oracle provides profound insight that complements the snapshot provided by aura photography.

Simply working through an issue or experience conversationally would very often lead to a solution or insightful revelation. Sharing and relating similar experiences is powerful and doesn't require fixing anything—it requires only listening and compassion.

PART 2: AURA WEAVING

CHAPTER 6

Aura Weaving 101

Aura Weaving is a metaphysical energy healing practice that uses the aura as a guide to align you with your life's purpose, allowing you to experience healing, abundance, and a deeper connection to the universe. Through this practice, you learn how to co-create, balance, and harmonize the energy field that surrounds you—your aura. It serves as your gateway to understanding and enhancing your emotional, spiritual, and physical well-being. In the exercises outlined in this book, you'll discover how to tap into the energy of your aura and use it to manifest your deepest desires.

In essence, Aura Weaving unfolds in a four-step process: first you'll learn how to channel energy; next we'll explore the colors, layers, and chakras of the aura; then you'll dive into the specific Aura Weaving exercises; and finally you'll learn how to weave your energy field to intertwine your unique powers and dreams. This method empowers you to interact with your aura in ways that support your healing, growth, and alignment with your life's purpose. Through this process, you will discover how to cocreate your reality with the universe, aligning your energy with your intentions.

Simply put, the Aura Weaving process is:

STEP 1: Learn to channel
STEP 2: Embody the aura colors, layers, and chakras
STEP 3: Learn the Aura Weaving exercises
STEP 4: Weave the aura to manifest your unique powers and dreams

By exploring practices such as visualization, meditation, and working with sacred objects, you'll develop a stronger connection to your personal energy field. The aim is to bring your aura into alignment with the energies of the universe, manifesting outcomes that enhance your life and deepen your sense of purpose. Your aura is constantly shifting and evolving with your emotional and spiritual states, and Aura Weaving offers a tool for actively engaging with and shaping this energy field.

This practice guides you toward becoming more attuned to the ebb and flow of your auric field. Whether you choose to follow the step-by-step approach or dive into the sections that call to you, the techniques offered in this book will help you tap into the power of your aura, aligning your life with your highest potential.

You might think that aura work or energy healing is reserved for those with rare gifts or deep esoteric knowledge, but that's not the case. You are already filled with magic, existing as a part of the cosmic web that weaves through the universe. By working with your aura, you can tap into that magic in a meaningful and transformative way.

Aura Weaving is both a new and an ancient practice that invites you to explore the intricate layers of your energy field. In the first part of this book, we explored the history and understanding of the aura, revealing how it has been perceived across time and cultures. The second part invites you to engage directly with your aura, using this knowledge to cocreate a life that is aligned with your true purpose. This is not about predicting the future but rather about understanding the energy you carry, seeing how it weaves together, and using that awareness to manifest your unique path. Aura Weaving is a cocreative process with the universe and an ongoing journey of self-discovery.

This section of the book is designed to empower you, offering the tools and knowledge to actively shape the energies that radiate from you, turning them into a force for achieving fulfillment and manifesting your truth. Please take your time and enjoy the process!

The energy of the aura is dynamic; it changes according to the emotions and lifestyle of the person who generates it, reacting to the physical and spiritual world in equal measure. But we are here to share a technique that will help you interact with the aura, effectively changing its appearance, which in turn can positively affect your life. This technique is Aura Weaving.

This practice guides your awareness to the delicate ebb and flow of the auric energy field enveloping you. This awareness forms the foundation for cultivating a sense of your energy's texture. You will learn how to stay attuned to your auric flow, and the sessions will act as touchstones for alignment with your authentic self.

Aura Weaving Framework

Aura Weaving is an art that transcends mere observation of the colors in our aura. It is a dynamic process of engaging with these colors to understand and transform our lives. The colors in your aura are not fixed destinations but guideposts on a journey of self-discovery. They reveal who you are in this moment, reflecting your current state of being.

Aura Weaving connects our visual sense with the subtle auric energy composed of our suppressed emotions and deep, unrealized desires. By building this bridge, we amplify our inner wisdom, gaining access to profound insights for personal growth, healing, direction, and self-understanding. Aura Weaving encourages a state of inspired action through a continuous cycle of intention, action, and reflection.

CHANNEL: The journey begins with learning to channel. In the next chapter, you will learn to open yourself to the flow of universal energy, allowing it to move through you. Channeling helps you connect with the higher vibrations and subtle energies that influence your aura. It's about tuning in, listening to your inner voice, and becoming a conduit for the wisdom that flows from the cosmos.

REVIEW: By applying your knowledge about colors, chakras, and aura layers, you will dig deeper into this practice. Each color and layer in your aura holds specific meanings, reflecting various aspects of your physical, emotional, and spiritual self. Understanding these elements helps you interpret the messages your aura is conveying. This knowledge is fundamental to the practice of Aura Weaving, as it provides the language through which your aura speaks.

LEARN: With a foundation of channeling and understanding your aura, you move on to the practical aspect of Aura Weaving. Learn exercises that help you interact with your aura, such as meditations, visualizations, and rituals. These exercises are designed to help you balance and harmonize your aura, enhancing its vibrancy and alignment with your intentions. This is about engaging in mindful actions that resonate with your inner self.

WEAVE: Finally, weave your aura to manifest your unique powers and dreams. This step involves setting clear, heartfelt intentions, taking inspired actions, and reflecting on your experiences. By continuously engaging in this cycle, you cocreate with the universe, aligning your energy with your life's purpose. This is where the magic happens—where your dreams begin to take shape, and your deepest desires become reality.

Setting a clear and conscious intention is the first step in Aura Weaving. This is not about setting rigid goals but about identifying guiding principles that resonate deeply within you. Your intention should reflect your true desires, thoughts, and feelings. As you become more aware, this intention can evolve, guiding your actions in a way that aligns with your authentic self.

The next step is to translate your intention into tangible actions. Engage in exercises that align with your intention, such as aura exercises, meditation, journaling, or other activities that connect you with your inner self. These actions should be mindful and resonate with your intention, helping you connect more deeply with your aura. Actions can also involve creative self-expression—through art, music, writing, or conversation—which allows you to express your true self and connect with others.

Reflection is crucial in Aura Weaving. It involves introspection and self-evaluation, helping you understand your progress and informing your next steps. By examining your values, motivations, and actions, you uncover layers of conditioning that may obscure your true essence. Reflection allows you to appreciate your journey and adjust your intentions as needed. Marking significant accomplishments with a ceremony can enhance this reflective process.

Aura Weaving is about creating a harmonious relationship between your aura and the universe, facilitating the manifestation of your deepest desires. By understanding and interacting with your aura, you can align your energy with your life's purpose, bringing about healing, abundance, and fulfillment. Embrace this journey with an open heart and mind, and allow the magic of your aura to guide you toward your true potential.

Through this process, you will discover how to articulate and set powerful intentions and boundaries, directly influencing your energetic field. This intentional alignment connects your aura with your deepest desires and aspirations—a crucial step in shaping your energy field. The universe responds, resonating with similar energies, and helps harmonize your aura with your life's purpose.

Aura Weaving is a powerful tool for channeling creativity, where art, music, and even scientific discovery come to life through the harmonious alignment of energy. By tapping into your aura, you can access deeper layers of inspiration, allowing the flow of creativity to move through you more freely. The process of Aura Weaving helps align your energetic field with your creative intentions, bridging the gap between the unseen energy that drives your imagination and the tangible expressions of your work. Whether you're painting, composing music, or exploring scientific ideas, Aura Weaving can guide you to unlock new perspectives and enhance your ability to bring transformative creations into the world.

Weaving the Aura

Now that you understand the aura and how to attune to the subtle energies that surround you, it's time to discover what you can do with this newfound awareness. Your aura, an energetic field that encases your physical body, is not just a passive shield; it's a dynamic and interactive part of your being. It absorbs and reflects your emotions, thoughts, and experiences, and at times it can accumulate unwanted energies or blockages.

This exercise is designed to help you restore your aura, removing any stagnant or negative energy that may be lingering within your energetic field. Just as you regularly wash your physical body, maintaining the health and clarity of your aura is important. By doing so, you can enhance your emotional and spiritual well-being, improve your interactions with the world around you, and deepen your connection to your inner self.

Exercise Prep: Finding Your Personal Yes or No

If you are new to the concept of working with your intuition, we recommend learning to discern intuitive yes or no responses within your aura before attempting the Aura Restoration exercise. This can be a profoundly empowering tool, enhancing your decision-making process and aligning you more closely with your true path. Your aura holds insights that extend beyond the limitations of rational thought. If you are a complete beginner, please be patient and resist the urge to qualify your progress or compare it with others'. Many of us have gone through life ignoring our "gut feelings" and sending those impulses to die at the altar of the rational mind. Your intuitive spark may be flighty, but it will grow when nourished by your trust and patience. It cannot be forced. The good news is you can just trust the process and your intuition will follow.

Yes/No Exercise

To begin, find a quiet, comfortable space where you can sit or stand undisturbed. Close your eyes and take a few deep breaths, allowing yourself to relax and become present in the moment. Visualize your aura surrounding you, a luminous field extending a few inches from your body. Feel its presence as a warm, gentle energy.

Now, think of a simple question or decision you are facing, something to which you seek a clear yes or no answer. As you hold this question in your mind, tune into your aura. Notice any shifts or changes in the energy around you. An intuitive yes may feel like an expansion of energy, a sense of openness or warmth that flows easily and freely. You might experience a sensation of lightness or a gentle pull forward.

On the other hand, an intuitive no can manifest as a contraction within your energy field. You could feel a sense of closing off, a cooling or diminishing of energy, or perhaps a subtle pushback or weight. For some, it almost feels like their stomachs "drop."

Pay attention to these subtle cues. Trust what you feel, understanding that your aura is deeply connected to your Higher Self and the collective consciousness. It's important to approach this exercise without preconceived hopes for a specific answer. The key is to remain neutral and open, allowing your aura to communicate authentically.

With practice, you'll find that your ability to interpret these energetic responses becomes more natural and evident. As you continue this exercise, remember that the process is highly personal and intuitive. Your experience may vary each time, and that's perfectly normal. Trust your instincts, go at your own pace, and allow yourself to fully experience the sensations and transformations that occur. This is not just an exercise; it's a journey toward greater self-awareness and energetic harmony. Remember, the answers are always within you; sometimes you need only to tune in and listen.

Aura Restoration

1. **Preparation:** Find a comfortable and quiet space where you can sit or stand undisturbed. Take a few deep breaths to center yourself. Inhale deeply through your nose, hold for a moment, and exhale slowly through your mouth. Repeat this three times.

2. **Aura Exploration:** With your eyes closed, extend your hands in front of you. Slowly move your hands through the space around your body, exploring the different layers of your aura. Pay attention to any sensations or resistance you might feel.

3. **Identifying Disturbances:** As you move through your aura, notice any areas where you feel discomfort, resistance, or any unusual sensation. These could indicate blockages or unwanted energies.

4. **Encapsulation of Energy:** When you identify a disturbance, use both hands to gently encapsulate this energy. Imagine cupping it between your hands. Be gentle and mindful during this process.

5. **Decision-making:** Ask yourself or the energy if it's ready to be released. This is an intuitive process. You might feel a response in your body or mind. If it feels resistant or not ready, acknowledge it and move on. If it's ready to be released, proceed to the next step.

6. **Releasing the Energy:** If the energy is ready to be released, visualize pulling in bright, protective energy from the outermost layer of your aura. Imagine this energy as a bright, golden light. Use this light to surround the disturbance in your hands.

7. **Letting Go:** Gently push the encapsulated energy out of your aura. Visualize it dissolving into the light, transforming into positive energy, or returning to the universe. Take a deep breath and release it, along with the energy.

8. **Weaving the Aura:** After releasing the energy, there might be a sense of space or emptiness where it was. Imagine your aura as a fabric that needs mending. Visualize "sewing" or weaving this space back together. Use gentle, sweeping motions with your hands to smooth over the area, restoring balance and integrity to your aura.

9. **Final Steps:** Once you've addressed all noticeable disturbances, take a moment to feel your entire aura. It should feel lighter and harmonious. To conclude, take three deep breaths to ground yourself back into the present moment.

10. **Reflection:** After completing the exercise, you may choose to journal any experiences, sensations, or insights that arose during the process. Reflect on how your aura feels now compared with before the exercise.

Remember, this exercise is deeply personal and intuitive. Trust your instincts and what feels right for you during the process.

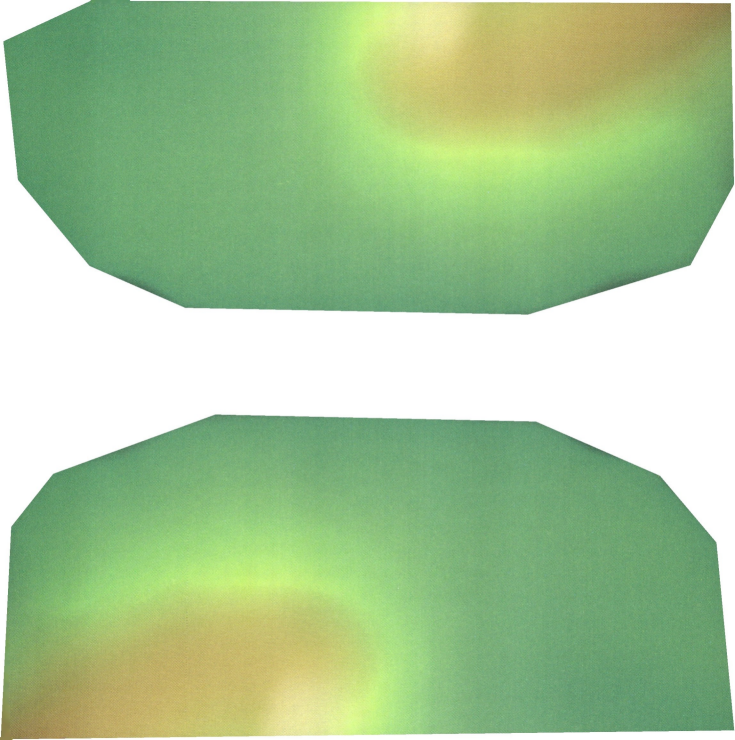

CHAPTER 7

Channeling

The practice of channeling energy serves as a bridge between the seen and the unseen, the material and the spiritual. Being able to channel is an important skill to hone to be able to weave the aura. We will learn to attune ourselves to the subtle vibrations of the universe and harness the divine flow of energy that surrounds us.

At its core, channeling energy is about connecting with the universal life force that animates all living beings. This energy, known by various names such as qi, prana, or ki, flows through every aspect of creation, binding us together in a web of interconnectedness. Through energy channeling, we learn to tap into this cosmic energy and direct it for healing, transformation, and spiritual growth.

The human aura, our intricate and dynamic energy field surrounding the body, can be conceptualized as a sophisticated antenna, finely tuned to interact with the diverse energies of the universe. Just as an antenna receives and transmits signals, the aura can be used to channel and manipulate various forms of energy, from the cosmic vibrations that influence our spiritual growth to the emotional frequencies that impact our interpersonal relationships.

By learning to perceive and adjust the frequencies of our aura, we can enhance its receptivity and effectiveness in channeling energy. This ability not only allows us to draw in nourishing energies that foster health and well-being but also enables us to project our intentions outward, influencing the world around us. The practice of tuning this "antenna"—through meditation, mindfulness, and, of course, Aura Weaving—optimizes our energetic interactions and alignment with our environment, leading to a more balanced, harmonious life.

The Wisdom of Ancient Channeling Traditions

Throughout history, various cultures and civilizations have preserved ancient wisdom teachings that offer profound insights into the nature of channeling energy and how it relates the human experience. These timeless teachings, passed down through generations, provide a roadmap for navigating the complexities of existence and uncovering the deeper truths that lie at the heart of our being.

In the East, traditions such as Hinduism, Buddhism, and Taoism include concepts that hint at the nature of reality, consciousness, channeling, and the human condition. From the concept of karma and reincarnation to the practice of meditation and mindfulness, these ancient wisdom traditions provide practical tools for self-realization and spiritual growth. The teachings of the Bhagavad Gita, the Dhammapada, and the Tao Te Ching offer wisdom that transcends the boundaries of time and space, guiding seekers on a journey of self-discovery and enlightenment.

In the West, traditions such as Hermeticism, Kabbalah, and Gnosticism offer esoteric insights into the nature of reality and the mysteries of existence. These mystical traditions delve into the hidden dimensions of consciousness, exploring the nature of the divine, the cosmos, and the human aura. The teachings of Hermes Trismegistus, the Zohar, and the Nag Hammadi library offer profound insights into the nature of reality, the nature of consciousness, and the interconnectedness of all things, inviting seekers to explore the depths of their own being and awaken to the divine spark within.

The Rainbow Body

Dzogchen, often translated as "Great Perfection," is a profound and ancient tradition within Tibetan Buddhism that emphasizes direct access to one's intrinsic nature. This nature is pure, luminous, and free from all obstructions, accessible through specific meditative and contemplative practices. Central to Dzogchen is the realization of the true nature of the mind, leading to profound liberation and enlightenment.

One of the most mystical outcomes associated with Dzogchen practice is the attainment of the "rainbow body," where an advanced practitioner's aura and physical body undergo a remarkable transformation. As the culmination of lifelong or even multi-lifelong spiritual cultivation, the practitioner's physical form dissolves at death, transforming into prismatic light and leaving behind minimal or no physical remains. This process signifies the ultimate purification of the aura, body, and mind, transcending physical materiality.

Achieving the rainbow body involves mastering practices that purify the aura and transform the energies of the physical body into the essence of the five elements: Earth, Water, Fire, Air, and Space. These elements are basic components of the physical universe. The transformation is often accompanied by the manifestation of miraculous phenomena, notably the appearance of rainbow lights around the practitioner, which are visible signs of the aura's intensified purity and vibrancy.

The concept of the rainbow body is deeply intertwined with the Tibetan understanding of the subtle body, which includes channels (*nadis*), winds (pranas), and drops (*bindus*) corresponding to the body, speech, and mind. Dzogchen practices focus on harnessing the winds and guiding them into the central channel, the most crucial pathway within the subtle body's aura. The

culmination of these processes allows the practitioner's body to transcend the limitations of physical form.

For adherents of Dzogchen, achieving the rainbow body is not only a personal sign of liberation but also a profound demonstration of compassion and the universal potential for enlightenment. It serves as a powerful inspiration for other practitioners, affirming the effectiveness of the teachings and the tangible reality of spiritual liberation.

In modern discussions within the Dzogchen community, the phenomenon of the rainbow body continues to be revered and discussed with mystical awe. It symbolizes the profound potential for human transformation and the ultimate unity of mind, body, and spirit within the electrified aura.

Across cultures and civilizations, ancient wisdom traditions, such as the rainbow body, offer a timeless roadmap for navigating the complexities of existence and uncovering the deeper truths that lie at the heart of our being. By studying and integrating these teachings into our lives, we can gain valuable insights into the nature of reality, consciousness, and the human experience, to have a better understanding of energy channeling and Aura Weaving.

Metaphysical Explorations

In addition to ancient wisdom traditions, modern metaphysical and spiritual movements offer a diverse array of teachings, practices, and perspectives on the nature of reality and consciousness and channeling. From the study of quantum physics and the exploration of consciousness through psychedelics to the practice of energy healing and intuitive development, seekers have a wealth of tools and resources at their disposal to deepen their understanding and experience of the secret.

Quantum physics, with its revolutionary insights into the nature of reality, has challenged our fundamental assumptions about the nature of existence. From the concept of quantum entanglement to the principle of non-locality, quantum physics suggests that the universe is far more interconnected and mysterious than we ever imagined. The study of consciousness and its relationship to the brain has also opened new avenues of inquiry into the nature of reality, suggesting that consciousness may be fundamental to the fabric of the universe.

Psychedelic substances such as ayahuasca, psilocybin, and LSD have been used for millennia by indigenous cultures for healing, divination, and spiritual exploration. In recent years, scientific research into the therapeutic potential of psychedelics has shown promising results for treating a range of mental health conditions, including depression, anxiety, and PTSD. These substances offer profound insights into the nature of consciousness and reality, opening doors to altered states of perception and expanded states of awareness.

Energy healing modalities such as Reiki, qigong, and Pranic Healing also offer powerful tools for balancing and harmonizing the body's aura energy systems. By working with the subtle energies that flow through the body, practitioners can facilitate healing on physical, emotional, mental, and spiritual levels, restoring balance and vitality to the mind, body, and spirit.

Intuitive development practices such as meditation, visualization, and intuitive journaling offer practical tools for accessing higher states of awareness and connecting with the wisdom of the soul. By quieting the mind and tuning into the inner guidance of intuition, seekers can gain valuable insights into their lives, relationships, and spiritual path, empowering them to make informed decisions and live authentically. These practices offer a direct pathway to the soul, inviting seekers to explore the depths of their own being and awaken to the infinite wisdom that lies within.

As we explore the vast terrain of metaphysical exploration, we are invited to expand our awareness, broaden our perspective, and embrace the infinite possibilities that lie beyond the horizon of our understanding. By integrating these teachings, practices, and perspectives into our lives, we can deepen our understanding of the nature of reality and consciousness and embark on a journey of self-discovery and spiritual growth.

How to Channel Energy

When practicing channeling energy, we may begin to experience profound shifts in consciousness and perception. We may feel a sense of expansion and interconnectedness with all of creation, as we realize that we are not separate from the universe, but rather an integral part of its divine spider-web. In moments of deep meditation or ecstatic bliss, we may even experience a merging of our individual consciousness with the universal mind, transcending the boundaries of time and space.

However, it is important to approach the practice of channeling energy with humility, reverence, and discernment. Although exploring consciousness can lead to profound insights and experiences, it can also be fraught with challenges and pitfalls. It is essential to cultivate a strong foundation of self-awareness, grounding, and ethical conduct, to ensure that our journey remains one of growth, healing, and service to others.

One of the fundamental aspects of channeling energy is cultivating awareness, protection and presence. Through mindfulness practices, we learn to bring our attention fully into the present moment, allowing us to attune ourselves to the subtle vibrations of energy that surround us. By practicing mindfulness in our daily lives, we become more attuned to the flow of energy within and around us, enabling us to channel it with greater ease and precision.

Developing Intuition

Another important aspect of channeling energy is developing sensitivity and intuition. As we deepen our connection with the universal life force, we may find that our intuitive abilities become heightened, allowing us to sense and perceive subtle shifts in energy that are not immediately apparent to the physical senses. Through practices such as energy scanning, aura reading, and intuitive meditation, we can learn to discern the subtle nuances of energy and gain valuable insights into our own energetic state and that of others.

In addition to energy scans, mindfulness, and intuition, the practice of channeling energy also requires a deep sense of trust and surrender. It is important to trust in the wisdom of the universe and surrender to the flow of energy, allowing it to guide and support us on our journey. By letting go of the need to control or manipulate the energy, we create space for the divine to work through us, facilitating healing, transformation, and spiritual growth.

One powerful technique for channeling energy is the use of intention setting and visualization. By setting clear intentions and visualizing the desired outcome, we can direct the flow of energy with focused intention and purpose. Whether we are seeking healing, clarity, or spiritual awakening, the power of intention can help us to align our energy with our deepest desires, manifesting them into reality with grace and ease.

We are merely vessels for the divine energy to flow through. It is essential to remain open, receptive, and aligned with the highest good. By cultivating a deep sense of reverence for the sacredness of the energy that we channel, we honor the interconnected web of life and contribute to the collective evolution of consciousness.

Energy Scanning

A body scan is a mindfulness practice that involves paying attention to parts of the body and bodily sensations in a gradual sequence from head to toe. When incorporating the aura into a body scan, the practice extends beyond the physical body to include an awareness of the energetic field surrounding it. Here's a brief guide on how to conduct a body scan that includes the aura:

1. **Find a Quiet Space:** Begin by finding a quiet and comfortable place where you won't be interrupted. You can either sit in a comfortable chair or lie on your back.

2. **Start with Deep Breathing:** Close your eyes and take a few deep breaths. As you inhale, imagine drawing calmness into your body, and as you exhale, imagine releasing tension and stress.

3. **Scan Your Physical Body:** Start the scan at the top of your head and slowly move your focus downward. Pay attention to each part of your body in turn—from the top of your head, down to your neck, shoulders, arms, chest, abdomen, back, hips, legs, and finally to your toes. Notice any sensations, tension, or discomfort.

4. **Shift Focus to Your Aura:** Once you have scanned your physical body, expand your awareness to the space around your body. Imagine a glowing light or energy field surrounding you. This is your aura. Notice the texture, color, and any sensations you feel in this space. Is it warm or cool? Vibrant or dull? Smooth or patchy?

5. **Scan the Layers of Your Aura:** Start close to your skin and gradually move your awareness outward. The aura has multiple layers, each extending a few inches to a few feet away from your body. As you move your attention through

these layers, be mindful of any emotional or energetic sensations. These might feel different from the physical sensations noticed earlier.

6. **Identify and Release:** As you notice areas of tension or blockages in your aura, take a moment to focus on them. Breathe into these spaces and imagine them loosening and releasing their energy as you exhale.

7. **Close with Gratitude:** Once you've completed the scan, take a few moments to thank yourself for dedicating time to your well-being. Slowly bring your awareness back to your surroundings and open your eyes when you're ready.

This practice can be particularly effective for identifying and addressing areas of emotional and energetic stagnation and can help promote a sense of overall well-being. Regular body scans including the aura can deepen your self-awareness and enhance your connection to both your physical and energetic bodies.

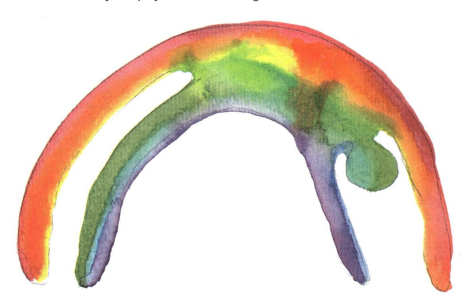

Channeling Aura Energy

The purpose of this exercise is to develop the ability to consciously channel and manipulate aura energy for self-healing, balance, and vitality.

1. **Find a Quiet Space:** Choose a quiet and comfortable space where you won't be disturbed. Sit or lie down in a relaxed position with your spine comfortably aligned.

2. **Center Yourself:** Close your eyes and take a few deep breaths to center yourself. Allow your body to relax and release any tension or stress you may be holding.

3. **Connect with Your Aura:** Visualize a bright, radiant, luminous egg surrounding your body. This light represents your aura, a vibrant energy field that extends beyond your physical form.

4. **Intention Setting:** Set your intention to channel and work with your aura energy for healing and balance. Focus on a specific area of your body or aspect of your well-being that you would like to address.

5. **Channeling Energy:** With your intention in mind, begin to visualize energy flowing from your surroundings into your body. Imagine this energy entering through the crown of your head and filling your entire being with warmth and light.

6. **Directing the Energy:** Once you feel the energy flowing within you, begin to direct it to the specific area or aspect you wish to address. Use your breath and visualization to guide the energy to where it is needed most.

7. **Sensory Awareness:** As you channel the energy, pay attention to any sensations or changes you may experience in the targeted area. Notice any shifts in temperature, tingling sensations, or feelings of relaxation and relief.

8. **Affirmations:** While channeling the energy, repeat positive affirmations or healing statements related to the area you are focusing on. Affirmations can help reinforce your intention and amplify the healing process.

9. **Gratitude and Integration:** After channeling the energy for a few minutes, take a moment to express gratitude for the healing energy flowing through you. Visualize the energy integrating with your aura and bringing balance and vitality to your entire being.

10. **Closing:** When you feel complete, slowly bring your awareness back to your physical body. Take a few deep breaths and gently open your eyes. Reflect on your experience and any insights or sensations you may have received.

Tips

- Trust your intuition and allow the energy to guide you during the exercise.
- Experiment with different visualization techniques and hand gestures to enhance your ability to channel energy.
- Practice regularly to strengthen your connection with your aura and refine your channeling skills.
- Be patient and compassionate with yourself throughout the process. Honor your unique journey of self-discovery and healing.

MODALITIES THAT ENHANCE AURA WEAVING

Try one of the practices below to complement your Aura Weaving work.

Reiki Healing

Reiki is a Japanese healing technique that involves the channeling of universal life force energy through the practitioner's hands to promote healing and balance. Practitioners receive attunements that enhance their ability to channel Reiki energy, allowing them to facilitate healing on physical, emotional, mental, and spiritual levels. Reiki sessions typically involve laying hands on or above the recipient's body, directing energy to areas of imbalance or discomfort.

Qigong Practices

Qigong is a Chinese energy cultivation practice that combines movement, breathwork, and meditation to balance and harmonize the body's energy systems. Through gentle movements and flowing sequences, practitioners learn to circulate qi (life force energy) throughout the body, clearing blockages and promoting vitality and well-being. Qigong practices can include standing postures, flowing movements, and guided meditations designed to cultivate awareness and sensitivity to energy flow.

Pranic Healing Techniques

Pranic Healing is a system of energy healing developed by Master Choa Kok Sui that utilizes prana, or life force energy, to cleanse, energize, and balance the body's energy centers, known as chakras. Practitioners use specific hand gestures, called sweeping, to remove stagnant or congested energy from the energy body, followed by techniques to energize and balance the chakras. Pranic Healing sessions can be conducted in person or remotely, and practitioners often use their hands to scan the energy field for areas of imbalance.

Crystal Healing

Crystal healing involves using crystals and gemstones to channel and amplify energy for healing and transformation. Each crystal has its unique vibrational frequency and healing properties, which can be used to target specific areas of imbalance in the energy body. Practitioners may place crystals on or around the body during a healing session or use them in meditation to enhance energetic attunement and alignment.

Sound Healing

Sound healing utilizes the power of sound vibrations to influence the body's energy field and promote healing and relaxation. Instruments such as singing bowls, tuning forks, drums, and voice are used to produce specific frequencies and tones that resonate with the body's energy centers. Sound vibrations can help clear blockages, release tension, and restore balance to the energy body, creating a sense of harmony and well-being.

Intuitive Energy Healing

Intuitive energy healing combines intuitive guidance with energy healing techniques to address the root causes of physical, emotional, and spiritual imbalances. Practitioners may use their intuitive abilities to identify areas of energetic congestion or disharmony and then channel healing energy to facilitate release and transformation. Intuitive energy healing sessions often involve a combination of hands-on healing, guided visualization, and intuitive insights to support the client's healing journey.

Energy Clearing and Protection

Energy clearing and protection practices are essential for maintaining energetic hygiene and safeguarding against external influences. Techniques such as smudging with sage or palo santo, visualizing a protective bubble of light around oneself, and setting energetic boundaries can help clear negative energy and shield against unwanted influences. Regular energetic hygiene practices are crucial for maintaining balance and well-being in the face of daily stressors and challenges.

Meditation

Meditation serves as a foundational practice for channeling energy, offering a sacred space for quiet reflection and inner exploration. We are also cultivating the temperament of our will. In the context of mindfulness meditation, especially within a sangha, the practice is not only about individual insight but also about shared spiritual growth. Rooted in the teachings of the Buddha, mindfulness meditation, or Vipassana, encourages us to observe the present moment without attachment or judgment, fostering both personal and communal harmony.

What the Buddhist calls the "monkey mind" is the constantly thinking mind. It is a mind relentlessly quantifying and labeling everything and everyone around us. When we sit to practice mindfulness meditation, we stop trying to subdue the monkey mind with distractions and substances and instead invite the monkey mind to participate with us in an activity: we simply sit, with a gentle awareness on our breath. The "monkey" will hate this, and conjure all manner of pop songs, recent arguments with family members, or enticing entertainments to engage the deeply engrained brain chemistry patterns. The astute mindfulness practitioner reserves all judgment of the monkey's temperament and instead labels all thoughts that arise as from the monkey mind as "thinking" and returns our attention to the breath. In this analogy, we are handing the monkey mind a toy—the breath. At first, he will fiddle with that toy for a moment and then immediately throw it down in search of something more stimulating. At that point, our astute practitioner, once again, will gently bring the monkey mind's attention back to the breath while labeling any distractions as "thinking." This is the practice.

As we practice, we open ourselves to the flow of energy by removing the obstructions of societal and cultural conditioning. In the stillness of meditation, we become deeply attuned to the subtle sensations and movements within our energetic body. This process enhances our awareness of the ebb and flow of energy, allowing us to notice the shifts in our physical, emotional, and spiritual states. We are cultivating a mind less conditioned to seeking of pleasure and avoidance of pain. This "grasping and aversion" is seen in Buddhism as the root of suffering. It is seen as a foundational approach that undergirds all paths to self-realization and enlightenment.

Additionally, in Southeast Asian and East Asian traditions, certain forms of meditation, such as Metta Bhavana (loving-kindness meditation), are practiced cultivating compassion and loving-kindness toward oneself and all sentient beings. This aligns with the heart-centered energy flow, particularly beneficial for balancing the Heart Chakra. Through this practice, we allow the energy of compassion to expand, harmonizing our personal aura and promoting emotional healing.

As we meditate, we also bring mindfulness to the impermanence of energy within us—how it constantly shifts and transforms, much like our thoughts and emotions. This insight into the impermanent nature of all phenomena helps us release attachment and allows for deeper self-awareness and peace.

Breathwork

Breathwork is another powerful tool for channeling energy. The breath serves as a bridge between the physical and spiritual realms. Through conscious breathing techniques such as pranayama or qigong, we can regulate the flow of energy in our body and cultivate a deeper connection with the universal life force. By aligning our breath with the rhythm of the universe, we synchronize our energy with the divine flow, opening ourselves to profound states of relaxation, clarity, and awareness.

Visualization

The power of the mind can shape our reality. By visualizing vibrant, healing energy flowing through our body, we can clear blockages, balance our chakras, and restore harmony to our energetic system. Using symbols, colors, and imagery, we can communicate with the subconscious mind and evoke profound states of healing and transformation.

Incorporating these specific techniques and practices into your daily routine can help you deepen your connection with the universal life force energy and enhance your ability to channel and work with energy for healing, transformation, and spiritual growth. As you explore and integrate these practices into your life, you may experience profound shifts in consciousness and embody the fullness of your divine potential.

Protection While Channeling

Channeling aura energy involves tuning into and manipulating the subtle energy fields that envelop and permeate the human body. Given the profound nature of this practice, it is crucial to employ protective measures to maintain the integrity and health of your aura. Engaging with energy without adequate protection can expose practitioners to negative energies that may cling to or penetrate their aura, causing emotional, mental, and physical imbalances. Furthermore, intense energy interactions can lead to psychic overload, resulting in symptoms such as fatigue, confusion, or emotional instability. Protection helps regulate the flow of energy and maintains personal energetic boundaries, essential for differentiating between one's own energies and those of others, as well as preventing the internalization of external emotional and psychic debris.

Implementing protective measures includes several key practices: grounding, shielding, using protective crystals, regular aura cleansing, and invoking spiritual protection. Grounding is essential before and after sessions and can involve walking barefoot, visualizing roots extending into the earth, or meditating with grounding crystals like hematite or black tourmaline. Shielding involves visualizing a protective barrier around the aura—a bubble of light, a cloak of energy, or a disco ball—that filters out harmful energies while allowing positive energies to pass through. Crystals such as black obsidian, amethyst, and selenite can also be used for their protective properties, worn as jewelry, carried, or placed in the practice space.

Regular aura cleansing is important to remove any lingering negative energies and can be achieved through smudging, salt baths, or sound vibrations from singing bowls or tuning forks. Additionally, invoking spiritual protection through prayers, mantras, or visualizations can call upon spiritual guides, angels, or protective deities to assist in maintaining a clear and secure energetic space.

Incorporating these protective techniques ensures that practitioners' energies remain clean, clear, and vibrant, safeguarding their well-being and enhancing the effectiveness of their work with aura energies. Thus protection is not merely a precaution; it is an integral part of the energy channeling process that enriches the practitioner's overall experience and efficacy.

The Disco Ball Shield

This imaginative exercise aims to create a protective energy shield around you, visualizing yourself within a shimmering disco ball. This visualization helps deflect negative energies and maintain a positive, vibrant energy field.

1. **Find a Comfortable Space:** Choose a quiet, comfortable place where you won't be interrupted. You can sit in a chair with your feet flat on the ground or lie down in a relaxed position.

2. **Ground Yourself:** Begin by closing your eyes and taking several deep, slow breaths. With each inhale, draw calmness into your body, and with each exhale, release tension and stress. Feel your body becoming more relaxed and grounded with each breath.

3. **Visualize the Disco Ball:** Picture yourself sitting or standing in the center of a giant disco ball. Imagine this disco ball surrounding you completely, with its surface just inches from your body. See the mirrored tiles covering the ball, sparkling and shimmering beautifully.

4. **Activate the Disco Ball:** Imagine that each mirror tile on the disco ball is infused with a bright, protective light. This light is powerful and can reflect any negative energy directed toward you. Visualize the light growing brighter and stronger, energizing the entire disco ball until it glows vibrantly around you.

5. **Feel the Protection:** Focus on the feeling of safety and protection within your disco ball. Imagine the mirrored tiles reflecting away all negative energies, bouncing them off and preventing them from reaching you. Feel the positive, protective energy contained within the ball, enveloping you in warmth and security.

6. **Enhance the Energy:** With each breath, imagine drawing more light and positive energy from the universe into your disco ball. See this energy enhancing the brightness of the ball, making it even more powerful and protective. Feel this energy reinforcing your disco ball shield, solidifying your protection.

7. **Maintain the Shield:** Decide how long you want your disco ball shield to remain active. You can set an intention for it to stay with you throughout the day, or for as long as you need it. Trust that it will continue to protect you from negative energies as you go about your activities.

8. **Closing the Exercise:** When you feel ready, slowly bring your awareness back to your physical surroundings. Take a few deep breaths, and gently open your eyes. Move slowly as you return to your day, carrying with you the sense of security and protection from your disco ball shield.

This visualization not only serves as a fun and engaging way to protect your aura but also reinforces your energetic boundaries, allowing you to maintain a positive and vibrant energy field throughout your day.

Embracing Worthiness: You Matter

Embracing worthiness is a fundamental aspect of the journey of Aura Weaving, as it is the recognition and acceptance of our inherent value and divinity. It goes beyond the surface level of our physical bodies and acknowledges the depth of our being as divine expressions of the universe. This realization forms the foundation upon which we can build a life of abundance, purpose, and fulfillment.

At the core of embracing worthiness lies the practice of self-love. This involves cultivating a deep sense of compassion, kindness, and acceptance toward ourselves, and acknowledging our strengths, weaknesses, and unique qualities without judgment or criticism. Self-love is not about ego or narcissism but about recognizing our inherent worthiness and treating ourselves with the same kindness and compassion that we would offer to a beloved friend.

Cultivating Self-Love with the Color Pink

This exercise aims to enhance self-love and promote deep emotional healing by focusing on the color pink, which is associated with the Upper Heart Chakra. The Upper Heart Chakra is centered on self-care, compassion, and unconditional love toward oneself.

Materials Needed
- A few minutes of quiet uninterrupted time
- Comfortable sitting or lying position
- Optional: Pink crystals such as rose quartz, pink candles, or any pink object

Instructions

1. Prepare your space.
- Find a quiet and comfortable place where you won't be disturbed.
- You may choose to hold a pink crystal, light a pink candle, or have a pink object within sight as a focal point.

2. Relax and center.
- Sit or lie down in a comfortable position.
- Close your eyes and take several deep, slow breaths to help relax your body and mind.
- With each exhale, let go of any tension or stress.

3. Visualize pink energy.
- Begin to visualize a soft, nurturing pink light. Imagine this light slowly forming above you, radiating warmth and love.
- Picture this pink light descending toward you and gently enveloping your entire body. Focus particularly on the center of your chest, where the Upper Heart Chakra resides.

4. Activate the Upper Heart Chakra.
- As you breathe in, imagine drawing the pink light into your Upper Heart Chakra, located slightly above the heart. Feel it warming and opening with each breath.
- With every exhale, imagine any emotional blockages or pain dissolving, replaced by a soothing pink glow.

5. Make affirmations of self-love.
- While immersed in the pink light, begin to repeat affirmations of self-love and care silently or aloud. Examples of affirmations include:
  - "I am worthy of love and kindness."
  - "I accept myself unconditionally."
  - "I nurture my body, mind, and soul with love and respect."
  - "Each day, I am filled with more self-love and appreciation."

6. Deepen your connection.
- Continue to breathe slowly and deeply, letting the pink light grow brighter and more vibrant with each breath.
- Allow the feelings of love and compassion to fill you from within, healing and restoring your sense of self-worth.

7. Conclude with gratitude.
- As the exercise comes to an end, take a few moments to express gratitude for the healing and love you have experienced.
- Gently begin to bring your awareness back to the present moment.
- Open your eyes when ready, carrying a sense of peace and self-acceptance with you.

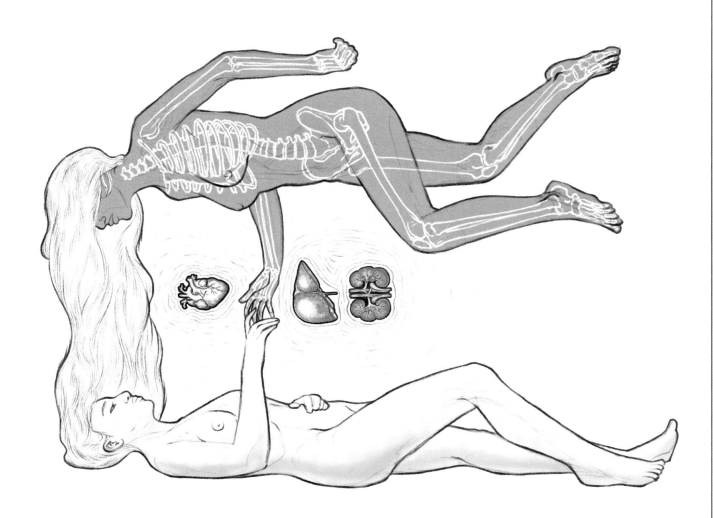

JESS'S STORY

Jess grew up under the shadow of an abusive parent, a reality that left deep marks not only on her heart but also on her aura. After moving away from her challenging home environment, Jess knew something had to change fundamentally for her to heal and move forward. She recalls the imagery of an aura photo taken in Sedona. The colors around her body were a dull and chaotic, reflecting her life.

It was during this transformative period that Jess discovered one of the tenets of Aura Weaving: meditation. Initially skeptical, she began practicing reluctantly, her sessions filled with the noise of intrusive thoughts and painful memories. However, Jess was determined and she persisted, weaving patience and compassion into her practice. Over months, her dedication began to bear fruit. The once-sporadic moments of calm during her meditations grew longer and deeper, allowing Jess to connect with parts of herself long silenced by her upbringing.

One day, while visiting a friend in Denver, Jess was drawn to Judah and Charlie's shop inside RitualCravt, where they offered aura photography. Curious and a bit nervous, she decided to try it, not sure what to expect. When her aura was revealed, Jess was astonished to see the radiant, vibrant hues of blue and green, colors that symbolize healing, peace, and growth. Charlie, noting Jess's surprise, explained that her aura showed significant signs of a person who was reclaiming their inner strength and nurturing their soul.

Seeing the tangible changes in her aura deeply moved Jess. It was a visual confirmation of the hard work she had put into her meditation practice and self-care. The aura photo motivated Jess to delve even deeper into her spiritual practices, exploring other methods of energy healing.

Through her continued efforts, Jess felt she had strengthened her sense of self-worth and autonomy. She learned to trust her intuition, guiding her decisions and interactions with a newfound confidence. And through her aura photo she was able to visually see how she was unlearning the limiting beliefs and patterns of behavior that no longer serve her and step into her own power.

MARK'S STORY

Mark worked in the tech industry, spending most of his days immersed in the logic of coding, problem-solving, and troubleshooting. Although his professional life was filled with data and algorithms, there was a part of him that longed for something deeper, something that didn't fit neatly into a spreadsheet or a code. Mark had always been skeptical about anything spiritual or metaphysical, but after a stressful period at work, a friend convinced him to try aura photography as a way to relax and explore something new.

Walking into RitualCravt, a metaphysical boutique in Colorado where we often conduct readings, Mark initially felt out of place among the crystals and incense. But he decided to keep an open mind. When he saw the photograph of his aura, he was surprised by the mix of electric blues and sharp reds surrounding him. Charlie explained that the blue represented Mark's intellectual side, while the red signified his underlying stress and frustration. It was as though the image had captured the tension between his analytical nature and the emotional toll of his fast-paced job.

Mark left the session with a lot to think about. He couldn't deny that the aura photo had accurately reflected his state of mind, and it made him realize how much he had been neglecting his emotional well-being. Inspired by the experience, Mark started incorporating small, mindful practices into his daily routine—taking breaks from screens, meditating, and allowing himself to feel rather than always analyze. Over time, these practices helped him find more balance, and he returned for another aura photo months later, eager to see how his energy had shifted.

SARAH'S STORY

Sarah had always been a practical, no-nonsense woman. Pregnancy, although beautiful, had come with its challenges—exhaustion, fear of the unknown, and a constant feeling of being unprepared. At eight months pregnant, she found herself at a crossroads. Her body was changing and, with it, her sense of control. She had heard about aura photography through a friend and decided, almost on a whim, to visit Judah's and Charlie's shop in Atlanta. "What could it hurt?" she thought, her curiosity laced with skepticism.

When Sarah's aura photo developed, it revealed a swirl of soft pinks and oranges, colors associated with love, nurturing, and creativity. But beneath the surface, there were clouds—muted shades around her abdomen, hinting at a deeper emotional block. Charlie gently pointed out that these colors often appeared in pregnant women, especially when fear and uncertainty were present. The Sacral Chakra, the seat of emotions and creativity, was calling for attention. Sarah had always been strong, but now she realized that she had been neglecting the emotional and spiritual bond she was building with her baby.

Moved by the insight, Sarah left the shop feeling as if a window had been opened. She began incorporating daily meditation, focusing on the light flowing into her Sacral Chakra, visualizing golden energy enveloping both her and her unborn child. Weeks later, she would return for a second photo, and this time her aura was clearer and brighter, as if the colors themselves had learned to breathe. For Sarah, the aura photo wasn't just an image—it was a reminder that her connection with her child was not just physical but deeply energetic, a bond that would guide her through birth and beyond.

CHAPTER 8

Spider Woman: Weaving Aura Power

In mythologies around the world, the motif of weaving is often linked to the manipulation of the aura and the fabric of destiny, embodied by Spider Woman, also known as Spider Grandmother, Arachne, and Neith, who each wield their looms and threads to influence the cosmos.

An Introduction to Spider Woman

In Aura Weaving, we are guided by the enigmatic figure of Spider Woman, a revered deity who embodies the interconnectedness of all life through her masterful weaving. Known in Native American mythologies under various forms—whether as the wise grandmother by the Navajo or the creative goddess by the Hopi—Spider Woman also mirrors similar figures in Greek, Roman, and Egyptian lore. In Greek mythology, she aligns with the skilled weaver Arachne, transformed into a spider by Athena; in Roman culture, she resonates with the tale of Minerva and Arachne, emphasizing themes of challenge and transformation; and in Egyptian traditions, we find her in Neith, the goddess who wove the world into being on her loom.

Spider Woman, in all her manifestations, serves as a guiding spirit, offering profound insights and practical techniques to enhance our energetic fields. Her presence across these diverse cultures enriches our journey, symbolizing the weaving of our personal destinies and providing thoughtful guidance. Her role ensures that we are skillfully interconnected with universal energies, enhancing our personal growth and spiritual connectivity.

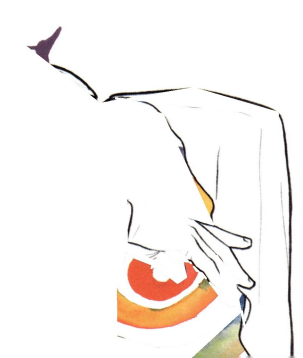

Spider Woman in Native American Mythology

Spider Woman, or Spider Grandmother, features prominently in Native American folklore, particularly among the Navajo and Hopi tribes. She is depicted as a deity of wisdom and a creator who connects all living things through her web, symbolizing the interconnected energy fields, or auras, that encompass and connect all forms of life. By weaving her web, Spider Woman balances the energies of the world, repairs broken connections, and communicates vital messages across the spiritual and physical realms, highlighting the profound impact of individual auras on the larger energy fields they inhabit.

Channeled Message from Spider Woman

In the sacred web of existence, there lies an insatiable curiosity, a deep yearning for knowledge and understanding that transcends the boundaries of time and space. From the dawn of human consciousness, this thirst has driven us to explore, to inquire, and to uncover the hidden truths that lie beyond the veil of illusion. You are now embarking on a journey of discovery, a path woven with threads of ancient wisdom and modern insights, stretching from the depths of the human psyche to the vast expanses of the cosmos. As you explore the realms of consciousness, you seek not just truth, but meaning, connection, and enlightenment.

    At the core of your being lies a fundamental drive to understand the nature of reality and your place within it. This quest for knowledge is not merely a pursuit of intellectual curiosity, but a deeply ingrained aspect of your humanity. Since time immemorial, you have sought to comprehend the mysteries of existence, grappling with questions that transcend the limitations of your finite mind. What is the nature of the universe? What is the purpose of life? What lies beyond the boundaries of your perception? These timeless inquiries have spurred you on a journey of exploration, discovery, and revelation, as you seek to unravel the secrets of the cosmos and unlock the mysteries of existence.

    Embrace the dance of creation, an intricate and profound journey of cocreation with the universe. Align your thoughts, beliefs, aura, and actions with your deepest desires to manifest your dreams and bring deep healing to the earth. This exploration of the subtle interplay between your inner world and the outer manifestation of your reality invites you to tap into the infinite creative potential that resides within you. Set your intentions clearly, take inspired action, and cocreate with the universe to bring your dreams to life. Trust in the wisdom of your aura and let it guide you on your journey toward self-realization and transformation.

In this sacred dance, you are not alone. The spirits of your ancestors, the wisdom of the ages, and the energy of the cosmos are woven into your very being. Trust in the web of life that connects us all and know that you are an integral part of this magnificent tapestry. Embrace your journey with an open heart and mind and let the light of your soul shine brightly as you walk the path of discovery and enlightenment.

Arachne: A Weaver of Destiny from Greek Mythology

In Greek mythology, Arachne was a Lydian woman, thought by some to be a princess, who was extraordinarily gifted in the art of weaving. Born to Idmon, a famous dyer in Lydia, Arachne's weaving was not just skilled but magical, turning each creation into a spectacle of beauty and intricacy. Her story is one of pride and transformation, as her ability to weave beautiful tapestries eventually led to a fateful contest with the goddess Athena, resulting in her transformation into a spider. This myth underscores the idea that the act of weaving can be a powerful metaphor for creating and altering realities, reflecting how practitioners might weave or reweave their auras to bring about desired changes in their lives.

Channeled Message from Arachne

Weaver of fate and tales, I once was mortal and now am entwined in the threads of the divine. In my mortal days, I defied the gods with my skill, only to be alchemized into the form of a spider, eternally weaving the web of existence. Through this transformation, I have come to understand the delicate interplay between the seen and unseen, the mortal and the divine.

Beloved weavers of destiny, to weave the aura is to engage in a sacred alchemy, transforming the raw threads of your energy into a tapestry of purpose and clarity. Authenticity is not merely a concept but a living, breathing essence that flows through you, guiding you toward your highest potential.

In the cacophony of the modern world, your aura stands as a beacon, a luminous guide to your true self. By finding your power in your aura, you peel away the layers of societal conditioning, revealing the radiant core of your being. Authenticity is not a static goal but a dynamic state of grace, a dance between your flaws and perfections, your light and shadow.

In your practice, let authenticity guide you. It is your compass, leading you toward integrity and resonance in all your interactions. It is not about achieving a fixed state but about flowing with the currents of life, embracing each moment with openness and love. In a society obsessed with image, your true self shines brighter than any facade. Beneath the layers of conditioning, your authentic self waits to be unveiled, a source of profound strength and joy.

By capturing the colors and patterns of your aura, your unique web, you gain a powerful tool for self-reflection and growth. This practice is not a linear journey, but a winding, spiraled path filled with revelations and transformations. It requires the courage to face your hidden depths, the vulnerability to embrace your true self, and the resilience to navigate the challenges along the way. Authentic living brings fulfillment, inner peace, and a deep connection to yourself and the world around you. Authenticity is not about perfection but about embracing your flaws and uniqueness with grace.

Your aura is both a mirror and a compass. It reflects your inner state and guides you toward experiences and relationships that resonate with your true nature. Honor the wisdom of your aura, and you will be led to people and places that uplift and nourish your soul, steering clear of those that drain your energy or compromise your integrity. Your aura is a testament to the substance of your being, guiding you away from societal illusions and toward your authentic path.

Remember, your aura is not passive but a dynamic participant in your journey. By cultivating awareness of your aura and trusting its guidance, you embark on a path of greater authenticity, vitality, and fulfillment. The wisdom of the ages calls to you: know thyself. Your aura is a living testament to this quest, ever-changing and ever-revealing the depths of your soul. Embrace it with grace and curiosity.

In this sacred dance of life, break free from societal constraints. Listen to the whispers of your soul, unlearn limiting beliefs, and embrace your unique worthiness. Reclaim your power and sovereignty, guided by your intuition and inner wisdom. This is the path, the alchemy of your being, leading you to your true self.

Know thyself.

Know thyself.

Know thyself.

Neith: The Egyptian Goddess of Weaving and Creation

In ancient Egypt, the goddess Neith was revered as the spinner and weaver of destiny, associated with the spider for her role in crafting the universe. As a deity, it was believed that Neith wove the entire world into being with her divine loom and that she daily reweaves the world, much like a spider consumes and reconstructs its web. This portrayal of Neith emphasizes the continuous creation and maintenance of the cosmic order and individual destinies, paralleling how individuals might manage their auras to maintain personal and communal well-being.

Channeled Message from Neith

Beloved children under the stars, I am the ancient weaver of the cosmos, the goddess who spun the very fabric of existence. In the days of old, I was revered as the Great Weaver, the one who threads the tapestry of life and death, of beginnings and endings. My loom encompasses the vastness of the universe, intertwining the threads of fate and destiny. Today I come to you with a message of profound transformation and connection.

To weave the aura is to engage in a sacred alchemy, a dance of energy that intertwines with the mysteries of the universe. It is an invitation to embark on a journey of self-discovery and connection, to delve deep into the depths of

your own consciousness, and to embrace your inherent worthiness. This practice is as ancient as humanity itself, a delicate balance of intuition and intention, where the seen and unseen realms converge.

Open yourselves to the divine flow of energy that permeates all creation. You become conduits for cosmic forces, guiding you toward deeper understanding and enlightenment. As seekers of truth, you yearn to uncover the secrets beyond the veil of illusion, exploring the vastness of your potential.

In my mortal days, I understood the importance of resilience and surrender. As I wove the fates of mortals, I saw the strength they gained by embracing their challenges and the wisdom they found in surrendering to the flow of life. Cultivating inner resilience involves developing self-awareness, self-compassion, and self-care. It requires you to nurture yourselves on all levels, strengthening your foundation for growth and transformation.

This path of transformation is profound alchemy. It transforms fears and wounds into wisdom and strength, awakening you to your true self. By honoring your worthiness, you reclaim your power to manifest your desires and create a life of abundance.

Cultivate resilience and surrender. Let go of attachments and trust the divine flow of life. As I wove the fates of mortals, I saw their strength in embracing challenges and finding wisdom in surrender. Your energy field reflects this journey, shining brightly with divine connection.

The process of embracing the shadow requires courage, compassion, and self-awareness. It involves shining the light of awareness on the parts of yourselves that you have kept hidden and exploring the underlying beliefs, emotions, and patterns that inform your behavior. By bringing conscious awareness to your shadow aspects, you create space for healing and transformation, releasing the grip of fear and limitation and embracing the fullness of who you are.

As you step into the fullness of your being, remember the ancient stories, the lessons woven into the fabric of existence. Your aura is not just a reflection but a powerful interface with the universe. By maintaining a vibrant energy field, you enhance your spiritual journey and contribute to the greater transformation of the world.

Embody the divine grace you aspire to. Shine your light brightly, and let your energy ripple through the cosmos, weaving a tapestry of love, wisdom, and transformation.

Weaving: A Universal Symbol in Aura Work

The stories of Spider Woman, Arachne, and Neith highlight weaving as a universal symbol of power and responsibility in shaping destinies. These mythological weavers teach us about the importance of nurturing and maintaining the aura, ensuring it remains a source of strength and harmony. In practicing aura work, one can draw inspiration from these figures, visualizing themselves as weavers of their energetic fields, carefully crafting and maintaining their spiritual well-being. Practitioners might use meditative visualizations where they see themselves weaving their auras with threads of light, repairing any tears and strengthening the weave, thus enhancing their ability to influence their personal energy fields and, by extension, their destinies.

Through these mythological lenses, weaving emerges not only as a craft but as a profound metaphor for the intricate work of managing life's energies and fates, underscoring the deep connections that bind the universe together and the powerful role of the aura in navigating these connections.

Spider Woman's lore beautifully illustrates the concept of the aura as a web of interconnected energy threads that encompass and connect all forms of life. Just as a spider weaves her web, Spider Woman weaves the spiritual and physical realms together, influencing the auras of all beings on Earth. Her web symbolizes the interconnectedness of individual auras and the collective energy field of the planet.

Weaving Aura Power, the Spider Woman Way

Spider Woman teaches that each thread in her web represents the aura of an individual life. She weaves these threads together, demonstrating how every being is interconnected. Her web reminds us that actions taken on one part of the web can affect distant parts, reflecting the impact of individual auras on the larger energy fields they inhabit.

Spider Woman uses her web to balance the energies of the world. She adjusts the tension and repairs threads, just as individuals must balance and heal their auras. By maintaining the integrity of her web, she ensures that the natural order and harmony of the universe are preserved, mirroring the way individuals must manage their auras to maintain personal and communal well-being.

In many tales, Spider Woman communicates through vibrations on her web, sending messages across vast distances. Similarly, the aura acts as a medium for psychic communication and intuition. By tuning into the subtle vibrations of their auras, individuals can receive guidance, perceive truths, and understand their connections to others.

Spider Woman's web also serves as a protective barrier, catching harmful energies or intentions that might disrupt the harmony of the world. In human terms, strengthening and cleansing the aura can provide a protective shield against negative energies, psychic attacks, and emotional pollutants.

Just as Spider Woman mends her web, she symbolizes the healer who repairs broken auras and restores spiritual health. Her actions teach the importance of ongoing aura maintenance—clearing blockages, healing leaks, and strengthening weak spots to ensure spiritual, emotional, and physical health.

To emulate Spider Woman's mastery over the aura, practitioners can engage in exercises that enhance their awareness of the interconnected energy fields around them. Meditation focused on visualizing the energy threads that connect one's aura with others can deepen understanding of interdependence and enhance one's ability to influence these connections positively. Regular aura cleansing, coupled with practices aimed at strengthening and repairing the aura, can mirror Spider Woman's meticulous care for her web, fostering a robust and resilient personal energy field.

Spider Woman embodies the power of the aura to weave connections, balance energies, offer protection, and facilitate healing and guidance. Her mythical web serves as a profound metaphor for the aura's role in the broader tapestry of life, highlighting the deep interconnections that bind the cosmos together. Through her stories, we learn the importance of nurturing and maintaining the aura, ensuring that it remains a source of strength and harmony both for ourselves and the world at large. If you let her work through you, magick will begin to unfold.

Channeling Spider Woman in Aura Work

In spiritual practices, "channeling" refers to the process of connecting with and embodying the energies or consciousness of spiritual entities, such as deities, spirits, or universal archetypes. When practitioners channel a deity like Spider Woman—a revered figure in Native American cultures, particularly among the Navajo and Hopi—they tap into her specific attributes and energies to enhance their aura work. This process can deepen one's connection to the cosmic web of life and enhance understanding of one's energetic impact within it.

Channeling Spider Woman involves embracing her embodiment of interconnectedness. In the context of aura work, this interconnectedness is not just a philosophical concept but a practical approach to understanding how individual auras interact within a larger network of life forces. By channeling Spider Woman, practitioners gain a heightened awareness of how their personal energy fields are woven into the vast tapestry of universal energies. This awareness helps them see the ripple effects of their energetic shifts on their surroundings and vice versa.

Channeling a goddess like Spider Woman means more than simply calling upon a mythical figure; it involves invoking and integrating her qualities into one's spiritual practice. Spider Woman is known for her skills in weaving, which symbolizes the creation and maintenance of life connections. When channeling her in aura work, practitioners focus on the active engagement of weaving and repairing their own auras. This includes visualizing their auras as part of a dynamic, interconnected web and actively working to strengthen and heal this web. Such visualization not only enhances the practitioner's aura but also contributes to the balance and health of the broader energetic environment.

Practical Steps to Channel Spider Woman

1. **SET AN INTENTION:** Begin your aura work by setting a clear intention to connect with Spider Woman's energy. This intention can be focused on learning from her wisdom in weaving the fabric of the universe and understanding the interconnectedness of all life forms.
2. **EMPLOY VISUALIZATION TECHNIQUES:** Imagine Spider Woman's presence and her intricate web. Visualize this web as extending from your own aura, connecting you to the elements around you—people, places, natural elements, and cosmic forces.
3. **MEDITATE AND INVOKE:** Use meditation to deepen your connection to Spider Woman. During meditation, you might recite invocations or prayers that call upon her guidance and wisdom, asking for her assistance in weaving your aura into the larger cosmic fabric.
4. **REFLECT AND JOURNAL:** After your meditation or visualization sessions, spend some time reflecting on the experience. Journaling about what you felt, saw, or received during the process can help solidify the connection and make the insights gained more tangible.
5. **MAINTAIN A CONSISTENT REGULAR PRACTICE:** Regularly channeling Spider Woman can strengthen your bond to her and make the insights you receive more profound. Over time, this practice can lead to a deeper understanding of how energies interact within your aura and across the broader energetic fields.

For someone new to these concepts, channeling Spider Woman in aura work is a way to actively engage with spiritual energies to enhance personal growth and energetic understanding. It invites a transformative exploration of how individual energies contribute to and harmonize with the universe's vast network, guided by the wisdom of a powerful and nurturing deity.

Weaving a New Reality

Of the transmissions in this book, this is by far the most important one. This exercise is designed to empower you to consciously craft a new reality by weaving energy within your aura. Using specific hand motions and focused intent, you will engage in a dynamic visualization process to manifest desired changes in your life.

1. Prepare your space.
Choose a quiet, comfortable place where you will not be disturbed. Ensure the area is conducive to meditation and free from distractions.

2. Relax and center yourself.
Sit in a comfortable position with your back straight but relaxed. Close your eyes and take several deep breaths. Inhale slowly and deeply through your nose, and exhale gently through your mouth. With each breath, feel your body becoming more relaxed and your mind more clear.

3. Set your intention.
Clearly define what you wish to manifest or change in your reality. It could be a new job, improved health, a sense of peace, or a relationship. Hold this intention firmly in your mind, focusing on the feeling of the desired outcome as if it is already happening.

4. Start weaving your reality.
Begin with your hands at the center of your chest, palms facing each other but not touching. Visualize a ball of light between your hands—this is the seed of your new reality.

Slowly move your hands apart, imagining that you are stretching and expanding this ball of light, making room for your intention within it.

Use specific weaving motions with your hands. Move them in and out, over and under each other, as if you are weaving threads of light. Each motion should be deliberate and focused, as you are building the structure of your new reality.

As you weave, visualize the details of your intention becoming clearer and taking shape within the aura of light between your hands. See the colors, feel the emotions, and connect with the energy of your desired outcome.

5. Energize your creation.

Once you feel that your weaving has formed a solid structure, place your hands over the ball of light and imagine it glowing brighter with every breath.

Visualize this light spreading out from between your hands and enveloping you, integrating your newly woven reality into your aura.

Say aloud or silently affirm that your new reality is now woven into your being and is manifesting in your life. You might use affirmations like, "I embrace my new reality with open arms," or "I am ready and open to receive these changes."

6. Close the exercise.

Gradually bring your hands back to the center of your chest and allow the visualization of the light to fade, trusting that your intention has been set and is now manifesting.

Take a few deep breaths, grounding yourself in the present moment.

Gently open your eyes and stretch your body, carrying the energy of your new reality with you as you move forward.

This exercise utilizes the power of visualization and the energetic sensitivity of your hands to mold and shape the aura, directing it toward manifesting your desires. Regular practice can help refine your ability to effect changes in your life, guided by the clarity of your visions and the strength of your intentions.

An Aura Weaving Session

Charlie here! When I lead an Aura Weaving session, it's an immersive experience where I guide the client through every step, working directly with their energy field to align them with their higher self and desired manifestations. The process involves a series of guided exercises, with each one tailored specifically to the client's unique energy. Here's a step-by-step guide on how I conduct the session, incorporating exercises from this book:

1. Grounding and Centering

I start by inviting the client to sit comfortably, and placing my hands just above their shoulders to tune into their energy. Together we focus on our breath, synchronizing until I sense their energy field stabilizing. This grounding exercise is essential before beginning any aura work. I visualize roots growing from the client's body, connecting them deeply to the earth. This helps solidify the connection between their aura and the physical realm. You can find a similar grounding practice on page 157, which helps calm and prepare the aura for deeper work.

2. Channeling Aura Energy

Standing beside the client, I hover my hands just above their body, feeling the energy flow. I guide them through a visualization, asking them to imagine a bright, protective light surrounding their body like an egg. As we continue, I channel universal energy through my hands into their aura, focusing on clearing any blockages or disruptions. This is when I invite the client to focus on their specific intention for the session—whether it's healing, clarity, or manifestation. Together we align their aura with their intention, making this a powerful collaborative moment.

3. Identifying Aura Colors, Layers, and Chakras

With the energy flowing freely, I begin assessing the colors and layers of their aura. As I move my hands over different areas of the body, I call out the colors and energies I perceive: "There's a strong blue in your Throat Chakra, which tells me you're working on communication," or "Your Sacral Chakra is showing a muddy orange, which may indicate a creative blockage." This part of the session is about using the aura as a diagnostic tool, helping the client gain awareness of their current energetic state.

4. Aura Weaving

With the client lying down, I start moving my hands in specific patterns above their body, pulling and stretching the aura's energy like threads of fabric. My movements are intentional, with each one designed to smooth out any disruptions or knots in the energy field. As I weave, I visualize their intentions becoming part of the very fabric of their aura, allowing them to cocreate the reality they desire.

In a session focused on manifestation, I often use the Weaving a New Reality exercise (page 182), guiding the client to actively participate in the weaving process. Together we visualize a ball of light expanding and contracting with each movement, representing their desires being woven into reality. This collaborative energy weaving strengthens the bond between the client's intention and their energetic field.

5. Sealing the Weave

Once the weaving is complete, I visualize the aura sealing. With deliberate movements, I smooth the edges of the client's aura, sealing in the energy and ensuring that everything we've woven stays in place. I focus on sealing any loose or frayed threads, reinforcing the intention and creating a balanced, harmonious energy flow. This step is essential in maintaining the integrity of the work we've done, helping the client hold onto the transformation that has taken place.

6. Final Grounding

To close the session, I visualize the color red to help guide the client back into their physical body. I place my hands on their shoulders and feet, gently pulling excess energy down into the earth, ensuring they feel grounded and stable. We take a final moment of stillness, allowing them to fully absorb the energy shift and reflect on the transformation that has taken place.

By the end of the session, the client's aura is harmonized, their intentions are woven into the fabric of their energy field, and they leave feeling empowered, aligned, and ready to manifest their dreams. The step-by-step process of Aura Weaving, as described in this book, creates a profound, transformative experience that not only shifts the client's energy but also aligns them with their highest potential.

CHAPTER 9

Advanced Aura Magick

By understanding channeling and learning how to work with the fundamental features of the aura, you have the tools to begin cocreating the life you desire with the universe. This chapter is all about seeing the aura from a different perspective, which will give you an even greater array of skills that you can use to work with aura energy.

In witchcraft, the aura is not just an ethereal glow but a gateway to profound spiritual insights and a tool for potent energy work. Witches use the aura to channel energy, cast spells, and gain insights into the unseen forces of the universe. By reading the colors, shapes, and vibrancy of the aura, they detect spiritual misalignments, identify energetic blockages, and tailor their magical practices, enhancing personal power and protection.

This chapter explores how witches, occultists, and spiritualists cleanse and shield the aura, channel energy during spellwork, and use the aura to amplify divinatory abilities and psychic development. Through these practices, witches turn the aura into an active part of their spiritual toolkit, allowing them to navigate the mystical realms with confidence and wisdom.

We will learn briefly about ceremonial magic, where the aura is a dynamic entity interacting with cosmic forces. Historical practices from ancient Egypt to the Renaissance reveal rituals like the Lesser Banishing Ritual of the Pentagram and the Middle Pillar Exercise, which cleanse, protect, and amplify the aura for higher spiritual communication and energy work.

Color magick also plays a crucial role in aura work, utilizing the unique energies of colors to influence and enhance the aura. Each color, from red's passion to blue's tranquility, can be used to invoke emotions, attract energies, and promote personal transformation.

By integrating witchcraft, ceremonial magic, and color magick, we can enhance our ability to weave the aura. By accessing deeper layers of magical power, we gain the ability to achieve personal and spiritual growth by fostering profound connections with the universe. Deliberate manipulation and harmonization of the aura enables you to navigate both the seen and unseen worlds with greater confidence and wisdom, embracing the full spectrum of your magical potential.

FROM CHARLIE:
A CEREMONY IN THE GODDESS GARDEN

In the heart of a lush, verdant garden, where the air was thick with the scent of blooming flowers and the whispers of ancient trees, a sacred initiation into the mysteries of the goddess Spider Woman unfolded. The Goddess Garden, a place steeped in magic and history hidden between mixed-use developments and massive breweries, was our sanctuary, a place where the veil between worlds was thin and the presence of the divine was palpable.

Leading our circle was Shasta, the revered crone whose wisdom was as deep as the roots of the oldest oak in the garden. By her side stood Shana, the crone in training, whose eyes sparkled with joy and mystery. Together with Cristiana and Esther, fellow priestess initiates, we gathered to embark on a journey that would bind us to the ancient web of Spider Woman.

We began by crafting our staffs, each one a unique extension of our spirit. The air was filled with the soft tinkling of bells as we adorned them, the sound weaving a delicate symphony that called to the goddess. Our hands worked with reverence and intention, threading ribbons, attaching crystals, and hanging charms that represented our personal journeys and the energies we sought to embody.

As the sun dipped below the horizon, casting the garden in a twilight glow, Shasta led us to the sacred circle. The earth beneath our feet was cool and grounding, connecting us to the ancient wisdom held within. We stood in silence, feeling the energy of the place seep into our bones, preparing us for the ritual to come.

With a voice that carried the weight of countless lifetimes, Shasta began to chant, calling upon Spider Woman to weave her web around us. The night seemed to breathe with us, each inhale and exhale syncing with the rhythm of the universe. Shana stepped forward, her voice joining Shasta's, weaving together a song of invocation that resonated deep within our souls.

Cristiana and Ester took their places beside us, forming a circle that pulsed with energy and anticipation. We lifted our staffs high, the bells ringing out in a harmonious call to the goddess. In that moment, the garden seemed to come alive, the shadows dancing and the stars above shining brighter as if bearing witness to our sacred rite.

Spider Woman's presence enveloped us, a warm and encompassing energy that spoke of creation, connection, and transformation. Shasta guided us through the initiation, her words of ancient lore and personal empowerment. We were asked to release our fears, to trust in the web of life, and to embrace the roles we were destined to play within it.

Before beginning the initiation, we activated our auras with the Light Prayer. This prayer, a central component of our Aura Weaving practice, called forth divine light to infuse our energy fields. As we spoke the words, we visualized our auras glowing brightly, each color resonating with our deepest intentions and spiritual aspirations. This activation prepared us to receive Spider Woman's blessings and heightened our sensitivity to the energies around us.

As we stood in the circle, we directed energy from our auras into the staffs, infusing them with our collective intention and the vibrations of the goddess. Each of us stepped forward in turn, speaking our vows and intentions—to Sekhmet, to Oshun, to Mary, to Spider Woman. As I stood before the circle, I felt the weight of Spider Woman's gaze upon me, a reminder of the interconnectedness of all things. My staff felt alive in my hands, a conduit for the divine energy that flowed through me.

When the final vow had been spoken, we anointed each other with sacred oils, sealing our initiation with the blessings of Spider Woman. The air hummed with our shared power, the garden itself seeming to exhale in a sigh of contentment. We had been woven into the web, our destinies intertwined with the goddess and each other.

As we left the circle, the bells on our staffs tinkling softly in the night, we knew that we had been forever changed. The bonds we had forged in the Goddess Garden would guide and support us, a testament to the power of connection and the sacred threads that bind us all.

The Light Prayer

The Light Prayer used in this ritual above is a sacred invocation used to activate and harmonize the aura, aligning it with the divine light and preparing the individual for spiritual work. It calls forth pure, radiant energy from the universe, infusing the aura with higher vibrations and enhancing its power for manifestation, protection, and healing.

Find a Quiet Space: Begin by finding a quiet and comfortable place where you can sit or stand undisturbed. Close your eyes and take a few deep breaths, grounding yourself in the present moment.

Visualize the Light: Imagine a brilliant, golden-white light above your head, representing the infinite source of divine energy. Feel its warmth and purity.

Invoke the Light: Speak the following words:

Divine Light, pure and radiant,
Descend upon me now.
Fill my being with your brilliance,
Illuminate my heart and mind.

Feel the Light Enter: Visualize the light slowly descending, entering through the crown of your head, and flowing through your entire body. Feel it filling every cell, infusing you with its healing and transformative energy.

Expand the Aura: Say the following:

Let this light expand and radiate,
Surrounding me with a protective glow.
My aura shines bright and vibrant,
Harmonized and aligned with the divine flow.

Set Your Intention: Hold the intention for the light to cleanse, heal, and empower your aura. You may focus on a specific area of your life where you seek guidance or support.

Seal the Energy: Say the following:

With gratitude, I embrace this light,
A beacon of love, wisdom, and might.
My aura is now activated and bright,
Aligned with the highest good, pure and right.

Feel the Connection: Take a few moments to feel the connection between your aura and the divine light. Breathe deeply, allowing this energy to integrate fully.

Close the Prayer: When you feel ready, gently bring your awareness back to the present moment. Open your eyes and carry the sense of light and harmony with you throughout your day.

The Light Prayer can be adapted and personalized to suit individual preferences and spiritual practices. It serves as a powerful tool for enhancing the aura, preparing it for deeper spiritual work, and maintaining a strong connection to the divine.

Magic Versus Magick

A note before we dive in: *Magic* and *magick* are terms often used interchangeably, yet they represent distinct concepts and practices. Although both involve manipulating energy and exploring mystical realms, they are rooted in different traditions and philosophies.

Magic, typically spelled with a final *c*, is commonly associated with stage magicians, illusionists, and performers who entertain audiences with tricks and sleight of hand. This form of magic emphasizes the art of illusion, where skilled practitioners use misdirection, props, and theatrical techniques to create the appearance of supernatural feats. Stage magic is often performed for entertainment purposes and is not believed to possess inherent supernatural or mystical qualities.

On the other hand, magick, often spelled with a final *k*, is a term frequently used in the context of witchcraft, occultism, and esoteric spirituality. Magick is understood as a practice of harnessing natural and spiritual energies to generate change in accordance with one's will. Unlike stage magic, which relies on illusion and sleight of hand, magick is believed to tap into the unseen forces of the universe, including the power of intention, symbolism, ritual, and the manipulation of energy. Practitioners of magick may engage in spellwork, divination, meditation, and other spiritual practices to manifest their desires, promote healing, or connect with higher realms of consciousness.

Although magic and magick share some common elements, such as the exploration of mystery and the use of symbolism, they diverge in their underlying philosophies and purposes. Magic tends to focus on entertainment and spectacle, whereas magick is often pursued as a spiritual or metaphysical practice aimed at personal transformation, empowerment, and the pursuit of deeper wisdom. Ultimately, whether one practices magic or magick depends on their beliefs, intentions, and the traditions they choose to follow.

How Witches Use the Aura

In the practices of witchcraft, the aura is viewed not just as a field of energy that surrounds the physical body but as a gateway to deeper spiritual insights and powerful energy work. Witches of various traditions use the aura to channel energy, cast spells, and gain profound insights into the unseen forces of the universe.

For witches, the aura reflects an individual's spiritual health, emotional state, and energetic potency. By observing and interpreting the colors, shapes, and vibrancy of the aura, witches can diagnose spiritual ailments, identify energetic blockages, and tailor their magical practices to address specific needs. This understanding allows them to enhance their personal power and protect themselves and others from negative influences.

Witches often integrate the use of the aura with other magical practices for enhanced effect. For instance, during sacred days called Sabbats or Esbats, witches might focus on aligning their aura with the specific energies of the celestial event the Sabbat recognizes, deepening their connection to the natural cycles and drawing down profound magical power.

In their work with deities or spirit guides, witches use their aura to create a compatible energetic space for communication. By aligning their aura to match the vibrational frequency of these higher beings, they facilitate clearer and more powerful exchanges.

In witchcraft, the aura is much more than a passive energy field—it is an active and dynamic part of the witch's spiritual toolkit. Through the deliberate manipulation and channeling of the aura, witches access deeper layers of magical power, protect themselves and their space, and connect more profoundly with the universe. This holistic approach to the aura enables witches to navigate both the seen and unseen worlds with greater confidence and wisdom.

AURA MAGNIFICATION TECHNIQUES USED IN WITCHCRAFT

Cleansing and Shielding: Witches often perform aura cleansing rituals to remove negative energy and spiritual debris that clutters the aura. This is usually done using tools such as herbs, crystals, smoke, or sound vibrations. Following a cleansing, witches commonly cast shielding spells over their aura to protect against psychic attacks and energy leeches.

Moving Energy: The aura is also used as a conduit to channel energy from the environment, deities, or the universal energy field. During spellwork or ritual, witches may draw energy into their aura, amplify it with their intentions, and direct it to manifest specific outcomes. This practice is often seen in healing work, where witches channel healing energy through their aura to the patient's aura.

Divination: Witches also use the aura to enhance their divinatory abilities. By attuning to the subtle shifts in their own aura or the aura of others, they can open channels of intuitive communication. This heightened sensitivity can enhance the use of tools such as tarot cards, runes, or scrying, providing deeper insights and more accurate readings.

Psychic Development: Through various exercises and rituals, witches work to expand and strengthen their aura, which in turn enhances their psychic abilities. Practices such as meditation, visualization, and energy work help refine their sensitivity to the energies around them, making it easier to perceive spiritual entities, auras, and magical currents.

CASTING PROTECTIVE CIRCLES: A WITCH'S METHOD FOR AURA PROTECTION

In many witchcraft traditions, casting a protective circle is a fundamental practice that serves to shield the practitioner's aura from external influences and to create a sacred space for magical work. This ritual is crucial for maintaining energetic purity and integrity, particularly when engaging in deep spiritual activities that might make one vulnerable to negative or disruptive energies.

The primary purpose of casting a circle is to protect the witch's aura from unwanted energies, ensuring that only beneficial forces are allowed within the sacred space. It

acts as a boundary that filters out external psychic noise and emotional debris, allowing the practitioner to operate within a clear and focused environment. Additionally, the circle helps to contain the energy raised during a ritual, enhancing its intensity and effectiveness before it is directed toward a specific intention.

How Witches Cast Circles

Choosing the Space: The first step in casting a circle is selecting an appropriate location where the ritual or magical work will take place. This could be indoors or outdoors, but the area should be quiet, undisturbed, and large enough to comfortably move within.

Cleansing the Area: Before casting the circle, it is important to cleanse the space physically and energetically. This might involve sweeping the area with a broom to remove physical debris and using techniques such as smudging with sage, sprinkling salt water, or ringing a bell to clear away negative energies.

Setting Intentions: The practitioner sets clear intentions for the protection and purpose of the circle. This might include the specific energies they wish to invite in and the energies they intend to keep out.

Marking the Circle: The circle can be physically marked on the ground using materials such as stones, crystals, chalk, salt, or herbs. Some practitioners use visualization alone, imagining a fiery or luminous boundary encircling the space.

Calling the Directions: Many witches call on the four cardinal directions—North, East, South, and West—often associated with elements of Earth, Air, Fire, and Water, respectively. This practice invites the energies or guardians of these elements to watch over and protect the circle, enhancing the aura's security.

Sealing the Circle: With the circle physically or visually marked and the quarters called, the witch then visualizes the circle being sealed. This might be imagined as a dome of light that encompasses the space, forming a protective bubble that extends above and below.

Activating the Circle: Finally, the circle is activated through an invocation or prayer, formally opening the sacred space. The practitioner might walk around the circle clockwise (also known as *deosil*) to raise energy and reinforce the circle's boundaries.

Once cast, the circle remains active until the witch's work is complete. Upon finishing, it is essential to formally close the circle, thanking any energies or entities that assisted in the ritual, and imagining the circle's energy being dissolved or grounded back into the earth. This ensures that the practitioner's aura returns to normal interaction with the world, retaining the clarity and focus gained during the ritual.

Casting circles is a powerful way for witches to protect their aura, focus their intent, and enhance their magical practices. By creating a boundary between the everyday world and the sacred space of ritual, witches ensure that their spiritual work is conducted within a sphere of safety and sanctity.

Ceremonial Magick and the Aura

Ceremonial magick, a tradition with roots extending back to the ancient civilizations of Egypt and Greece, encompasses a wide array of practices aimed at understanding and harnessing the unseen forces of the universe. Historical evidence suggests that as early as the second century CE, Egyptian priests performed complex rituals involving invocations and symbolic gestures to communicate with the gods. Similarly, the Greeks used forms of ritual magick for protection and divination, often invoking deities and spirits through elaborate ceremonies.

Over the centuries, these ancient practices were woven into a richer tapestry of ritual magic, incorporating elements from Kabbalah, a mystical form of Judaism that emerged in the twelfth century, and Hermeticism, which traces its roots to the writings attributed to Hermes Trismegistus during the Hellenistic period. The Renaissance period saw a revival and reinterpretation of these ancient arts, particularly influenced by figures such as Heinrich Cornelius Agrippa, whose work *Three Books of Occult Philosophy*, published in 1533, became a cornerstone of Western esotericism.

Central to the practice of ceremonial magick is the concept of the aura or the subtle body, which practitioners view as a dynamic entity interacting with cosmic forces. Ceremonial magicians, such as those from the Hermetic Order of the Golden Dawn, founded in the late nineteenth century, focused extensively on aura manipulation. They practiced rituals like the Lesser Banishing Ritual of the Pentagram, developed in the late 1800s, to cleanse and protect the aura, preparing it as a vessel for higher energies.

Moreover, the aura was used as a protective barrier and a medium for spiritual communication. The Golden Dawn, and later Aleister Crowley in the early twentieth century, emphasized the necessity of aligning one's aura with the entities summoned during evocations. Crowley's modifications to Golden Dawn rituals, which he published in works like *Liber O*, aimed at enhancing the practitioner's ability to control their aura for safer and more effective magical operations.

In modern times, the principles of ceremonial magick, enriched by new age philosophies and contemporary esoteric practices, continue to evolve. However, the foundational belief in the power of the aura remains central. Modern practitioners, drawing on both traditional techniques and innovative approaches, explore the depths of aura manipulation. They aim not only for personal empowerment and spiritual insight but also strive to achieve a harmonious balance with the universal energies that ceremonial magick navigates.

This detailed exploration of ceremonial magick's history and its complex use of the aura underscores a tradition both profound and potent, reflecting humanity's enduring quest to comprehend the cosmos and our place within it.

Spellwork in Ceremonial Magick to Electrify the Aura

Ceremonial magicians engage in a variety of exercises designed to magnify their auras, enhancing their energy fields for stronger magical workings and deeper spiritual connections. These exercises often combine elements of visualization, meditation, and the manipulation of elemental energies, providing practitioners with powerful tools to increase the vibrancy and reach of their auras. These exercises are very complex, so we provide a rough outline but further exploration is needed to integrate these into your practice.

The Lesser Banishing Ritual of the Pentagram (LBRP)

This foundational ritual in ceremonial magick is used both for protection and for clearing and strengthening the aura. The LBRP involves drawing pentagrams in the air at the four cardinal directions, invoking the archangels associated with each direction, and reciting specific Hebrew names of God. This exercise helps to purify the surrounding space and the magician's aura, creating a fortified, vibrant energy field that repels negativity.

The Middle Pillar Exercise

The Middle Pillar Exercise is designed to balance and expand the aura by stimulating the body's main energy centers (or Sephiroth on the Tree of Life in Kabbalistic terms). Practitioners visualize divine light descending from above into the crown of their head and flowing down along the central column of their body, illuminating five key points (the crown, throat, heart, solar plexus, and groin). This exercise not only enhances the aura but also helps in channeling higher spiritual energies into physical existence.

Circulation of the Body of Light

This exercise involves circulating light throughout the body and aura to fortify and cleanse it. Magicians begin by visualizing a brilliant light at the heart center, which expands to fill the entire body and then extends into the aura. This light is then circulated, often guided by the breath, moving in specific patterns that can include horizontal or vertical loops. This practice increases the vibrancy and elasticity of the aura, making it more receptive to magical influences.

Elemental Balancing Ritual

Understanding and balancing the four classical elements (Earth, Air, Fire, Water) within the aura is crucial in ceremonial magick. Practitioners may use a ritual involving the invocation of elemental energies, visualizing each element infusing their aura with specific qualities: stability from Earth, clarity from Air, dynamism from Fire, and fluidity from Water. By balancing these elements, the magician's aura becomes a harmonious and powerful conduit for magickal work.

Invoking the Higher Self

In this meditative exercise, the practitioner focuses on connecting with their Higher Self, a divine aspect of their being. Through deep meditation, they visualize their Higher Self as a source of brilliant light above them, gradually allowing this light to descend and fully integrate with their aura. This practice not only magnifies the aura but also aligns it more closely with the practitioner's spiritual purpose and potential.

Solar Adorations

Aligned with Hermetic traditions, solar adorations involve aligning one's energy with the sun at various points of the day (dawn, noon, sunset, midnight). The magician performs gestures and chants specific prayers or invocations that draw down solar energy into the aura, magnifying its power and brightness. This ritual connects the practitioner's energy cycle with the natural rhythm of the sun, enhancing personal vitality and magickal effectiveness.

These exercises are integral components of a ceremonial magician's practice, each serving to enhance and expand the aura in different ways. By regularly performing these rituals, magicians strengthen their energetic presence, refine their spiritual focus, and enhance their capabilities in both magickal and mundane realms.

Color Magick

Color Magick, an ancient and potent branch of metaphysical practice, has been woven into the fabric of spiritual and mystical traditions throughout history. Its roots extend back to some of the earliest human cultures, where color was not just an aesthetic choice but a powerful tool for healing, transformation, and ritual. Across time, from the Egyptians and their chromotherapy to the ceremonial magicians of the Renaissance, the use of color has been fundamental in shaping energy fields, invoking the divine, and altering the physical and spiritual state of the individual.

Today Color Magick plays a vital role in Aura Weaving, as it taps into the inherent vibrational qualities of different hues to influence the aura—a luminous field that surrounds the body. This field is not static but dynamic, constantly shifting and reacting to our inner and outer experiences. The colors of the aura offer insight into our physical health, emotional state, and spiritual well-being, and can be intentionally altered through Color Magick to achieve desired results. The long history of color use in ritual and spiritual practice converges here, in the modern understanding of how our energetic body can be shaped and guided through the intentional use of color.

The use of color as a mystical and healing tool can be traced back thousands of years. Ancient Egypt, for example, practiced a form of chromotherapy that relied on the healing power of different colors. Temples were built with specific rooms for healing, bathed in colored light that corresponded to different ailments or conditions. Red was believed to stimulate and energize, while blue calmed the spirit, promoting a state of peace and relaxation. This practice was deeply connected to their spiritual belief in the harmonious balance among body, mind, and the divine.

Similarly, in ancient India, the concept of chakras—energy centers within the body— became closely associated with color. Each chakra was aligned with a specific hue, forming a rainbowlike spectrum that extended from the base of the spine to the crown of the head. These colors were more than symbolic; they were energetic frequencies that could be activated or balanced through meditation, visualization, and the use of colored materials or lights. This understanding of color as an energetic force continues to influence modern practices of Color Magick and Aura Weaving.

Throughout history, colors have been revered not only for their aesthetic qualities but also for their ability to affect human consciousness. In medieval alchemy, for instance, the transformation of metals was often linked to color stages, with each one representing a deeper level of spiritual refinement. Gold, as the ultimate goal, was the symbol of enlightenment and the perfection of the soul, a concept that resonates with the modern use of golden light to manifest abundance and success in Color Magick.

The Renaissance involved a revival of esoteric knowledge and magical practices, including the use of color in ceremonial magic. Magicians and scholars of the time, such as Cornelius Agrippa, explored the power of color in conjunction with the planets, elements, and sacred geometry. Each color was believed to resonate with certain planetary energies and divine forces, and could be used to summon or direct these powers in ritual.

For instance, red was connected to the planet Mars, symbolizing strength, courage, and protection, while blue was associated with Jupiter, promoting wisdom, expansion, and prosperity. These correspondences laid the groundwork for the modern practice of Color Magick, where specific hues are used to invoke the qualities or energies they represent, whether in healing, protection, or manifestation.

As ceremonial magic evolved into more contemporary practices, the connection between color and the aura became more pronounced. The aura, now understood as a multilayered field of energy that reflects and interacts with our physical, emotional, and spiritual states, became a focal point for healing and manifestation work. Color Magick became a tool not just for ritual and spellwork, but for direct manipulation of the aura itself.

In the modern practice of Aura Weaving, Color Magick remains a key component. The idea that each color emits a specific frequency aligns with our understanding of the aura as a vibrational field. By intentionally working with different colors, we can shift and shape the energy within and around us, bringing our aura into alignment with our desired outcomes.

For example, during an Aura Weaving session, a practitioner might sense a blockage in the Sacral Chakra, represented by the color orange. To dissolve this blockage and restore balance, the practitioner could visualize a vibrant orange light filling the Sacral Chakra while guiding the client to engage in activities that stimulate creativity and joy. This deliberate use of color allows the aura to harmonize with the emotional and spiritual state that is being cultivated, resulting in a more balanced and empowered energy field.

The colors within our aura are more than reflections of our current state—they are gateways to transformation. By incorporating Color Magick into Aura Weaving, we actively engage with the vibrational qualities of color to heal wounds, release stagnant energy, and manifest new possibilities. The practice of weaving colors into the aura can be as simple as visualizing the desired hues during meditation, or as complex as integrating crystals, candles, and ritual objects of a specific color into the process.

Each color carries its own unique frequency and vibration that can affect our emotional, physical, and spiritual states in profound ways. When used intentionally, colors can shift our energy field, balance our chakras, and help us manifest our desires. Understanding the deeper meanings and effects of each color is key to effectively using Color Magick in aura weaving. Here's a more detailed exploration of how specific colors can transform your aura and influence your life:

- **RED:** the color of primal energy, life force, and raw power. It embodies vitality, courage, and action. In the context of Aura Weaving, red is essential for grounding, as it connects us to the earth and our physical bodies. It stimulates the Base (Root) Chakra, giving us the strength to overcome obstacles and face challenges with resilience. When your aura is infused with red, you might feel more energized, focused, and capable of taking decisive action. It also encourages passion, whether in love, creativity, or ambition. However, too much red can signify aggression or anger, so balance is crucial when using this color.

- **ORANGE:** the color of creativity, sensuality, and emotional health. It resonates with the Sacral Chakra and is tied to our ability to experience joy, pleasure, and connection with others. When orange is woven into the aura, it sparks inspiration, encourages a playful spirit, and helps release emotional blockages. Orange promotes self-expression, creativity in art and relationships, and a zest for life. It's also connected to sexuality and intimacy, helping to heal wounds in these areas. This color is great for anyone feeling creatively stifled or emotionally withdrawn.

- **YELLOW:** the color of intellect, mental clarity, and self-confidence. It is closely associated with the Solar Plexus Chakra, which governs personal power, self-esteem, and decision-making. Weaving yellow into your aura brings mental focus, optimism, and a brighter outlook on life. It clears away confusion and encourages assertiveness and confidence in pursuing your goals. If you find yourself in a fog of indecision or lacking motivation, yellow can bring the clarity needed to move forward. On the flip side, too much yellow can lead to overthinking or nervousness, so using it wisely is important.

- **GREEN:** the color of balance, growth, healing, and abundance. It vibrates in harmony with the Heart Chakra, making it the color of unconditional love, compassion, and emotional well-being. In Aura Weaving, green helps restore equilibrium in the energy body, especially if you are healing from emotional wounds or looking to manifest new growth in your life—whether in your career, relationships, or personal development. Green symbolizes harmony with the natural world and is also linked to financial prosperity. When your aura is filled with green, you may find yourself feeling more at peace, with a deep sense of connection to others and the world around you.

- **BLUE:** represents calm, communication, and truth. It is aligned with the Throat Chakra and governs self-expression, honesty, and clarity of speech. Weaving blue into your aura can help you communicate more effectively and peacefully. It also soothes anxiety and stress, promoting a sense of inner calm. Blue is often used in meditation to quiet the mind and encourage a deeper connection to the spiritual self. If you struggle with finding your voice or are in a time of confusion, blue energy can help you express your authentic self with ease and confidence. Too much blue, however, can lead to feelings of detachment or coldness, so balance is key.

- **INDIGO:** the color of intuition, spiritual insight, and inner wisdom. It aligns with the Third Eye Chakra, which governs psychic abilities, perception, and higher consciousness. When indigo is woven into the aura, it enhances your ability to see beyond the physical realm, allowing you to tap into your intuitive knowledge and gain insight into deeper truths. Indigo helps you connect with your higher self, guiding you toward spiritual enlightenment and a greater understanding of the mysteries of life. This color is particularly useful in meditation and divination practices, helping you attune to subtle energies and spiritual guidance.

- **VIOLET:** associated with the Crown Chakra, the color of spiritual transformation, divine connection, and purification. It embodies the energy of ascension and higher consciousness, helping to open the channels between the physical self and the spiritual realms. When violet is woven into the aura, it can cleanse and protect, purifying any lower vibrations or negative energy that might be clouding it. Violet helps you align with your higher purpose and connect with the divine, fostering spiritual growth and wisdom. It is also used for psychic protection and clearing energetic blockages, making violet a powerful color for deep healing and transformation.

- **PINK:** a color of unconditional love, compassion, and self-care. It connects with the softer, nurturing aspects of the Heart Chakra, encouraging empathy, kindness, and emotional healing. When pink is present in the aura, it signifies a state of openness to love and a willingness to nurture both the self and others. It is often used in aura weaving to heal emotional scars, foster forgiveness, and cultivate self-love. Pink is ideal for anyone seeking to heal their heart, whether from heartbreak, grief, or self-criticism. Its gentle energy promotes harmony in relationships and creates a sense of peace within.

Weaving Color Into Your Aura Practice

Incorporating Color Magick into your aura weaving practice is a dynamic and intuitive process. It involves engaging with the energetic frequencies of colors through various techniques that can shift your aura, bring balance to your chakras, and help manifest your desires. Here are some detailed ways to weave color into your aura practice:

- **VISUALIZATION:** This is one of the most powerful tools for integrating Color Magick into your Aura Weaving practice. During meditation or while in a relaxed state, visualize a specific color filling your aura or surrounding the area of your body associated with a particular chakra. For example, if you're working on self-confidence, visualize a radiant yellow light emanating from your solar plexus, expanding outward, and filling your entire aura. Let the color saturate your energy field, bringing with it the qualities you wish to embody.

- **CRYSTALS AND GEMSTONES:** These are potent tools in Aura Weaving because they naturally hold the vibrational frequencies of specific colors. Use colored stones that correspond with your intention, such as rose quartz for pink, amethyst for violet, or citrine for yellow. During a session, place these crystals on or around your body, focusing on the area of your aura you wish to balance or enhance. Their energy can amplify the effects of your color visualization and help restore harmony to your aura.

- **CANDLES AND LIGHTS:** Incorporating colored candles or lights into your aura weaving ritual can have a profound effect on the energy you are working with. Each candle color corresponds to a specific intention. For example, lighting a blue candle can enhance communication, whereas a green candle can promote healing and growth. As you weave color into your aura, focus on the flickering flame, imagining it feeding the corresponding color into your energy field. Colored lights in your meditation or ritual space can also set the tone and amplify the energy of the color you're working with.

- **CLOTHING AND ACCESSORIES:** The colors you choose to wear can have a subtle but powerful influence on your aura throughout the day. By consciously selecting clothing and accessories in specific colors, you can influence your aura and energy field. Wearing red can boost your vitality and ground you, and wearing blue might help you communicate more clearly and remain calm in stressful situations. This practice can be especially helpful when you need to reinforce a specific energy for extended periods.

- **ARTWORK AND AESTHETICS:** Surrounding yourself with intentional color choices in your environment—whether through art, decor, or objects—creates a vibrational field that constantly interacts with your aura. For example, placing green plants in your home not only brings the healing energy of nature but also the restorative power of the color green, influencing your Heart Chakra and overall emotional balance. Creating or collecting artwork that resonates with certain colors can also enhance the corresponding energies in your aura.

- **DAILY COLOR FOCUS:** A simple but powerful practice is to choose a "color of the day" and focus on embodying its qualities throughout your activities. Each morning, decide on a color that aligns with your goals or intentions for the day. Visualize this color filling your aura and consciously carry its energy with you as you go about your tasks. For example, if you need extra energy and motivation, focus on red. If you're seeking clarity and peace, focus on blue. This daily practice helps build a deeper relationship with colors and their impact on your aura.

By weaving these colors into your aura, you are actively participating in the energetic dynamics that shape your life. Through Color Magick, you become a conscious creator of your reality, aligning your energy with your intentions and enhancing your ability to manifest your highest desires. Whether through simple visualizations or more complex rituals, using the transformative power of colors can elevate your aura work and lead you to a deeper sense of harmony, healing, and spiritual alignment.

CONCLUSION

From the bottom of our hearts, we thank you for joining us on this journey of sharing our knowledge in our very first book! Remember to be kind to yourself on this exploration; there's no rush. You have your entire life to understand yourself. This book has not only explored the colors and contours of your energetic selves but also demonstrated how these insights can guide you toward living a life that is more aligned with our true essence.

When working with Aura Weaving, don't worry about finding definitive answers or solving the ultimate riddle of existence—just keep embracing the mystery of life itself. The Universe has its special ways to let you know it's listening. Remember that Life is moving through YOU and imploring you to discover yourself and what to do about it. Aura Weaving is about embracing the unknown, the unknowable, and the infinite possibilities that lie beyond our comprehension. Cultivate a sense of wonder. Live the Mystery. Surf that mystery.

Surrender to the flow of life, explore the present moment, and trust in the wisdom of the universe. Set your intention to navigate the complexities of existence with grace and ease, knowing that we are guided and supported every step of the way.

It is a journey of exploration and discovery that invites us to expand our awareness, broaden our perspective, and embrace the infinite possibilities that lie beyond the horizon of our understanding. By remaining open, curious, and receptive to the mysteries of existence, we can continue to deepen our understanding, broaden our perspective, and awaken to the boundless potential that lies within us and all around us.

We have seen how the aura serves as a mirror reflecting our deepest desires, fears, and potential. It can be used to reveal the core of our authentic selves. By engaging with our aura, we engage with the truth of who we are, beyond the roles and expectations imposed upon us by the outside world.

Each day offers a new opportunity to use the insights gained from our aura to foster personal growth and transformation. We encourage you to continue the practices outlined in this book: setting intentions, interpreting the colors and messages of your aura, and making decisions that resonate with your authentic self. These tools are not only for occasional reflection but for continuous application, helping you navigate the challenges and opportunities of life with the rhythmic framework of intention→action→reflection.

Acceptance is also about trusting that, even without seeing the entire map of our life's journey, we are exactly where we need to be. We are the expert of our experiences. See each color of our auras as a gift of insight and opportunity. Let go of the need for certainty and control, and instead cultivate a relationship with the unknown that is based on trust and openness.

As we move forward, let us carry with us the lessons of Aura Weaving—embracing our full spectrum of energies with acceptance and love, and using our understanding to not only better ourselves but also to contribute to the greater good. The journey of self-discovery through Aura Weaving is infinite; it is a continuous dance with the energies of the universe, a dance in which we are both participants and observers.

Remember that everything just might work out not because every part of the journey is predetermined, but because when we align with our authentic selves and trust in the flow of life, we are more capable of creating outcomes that resonate deeply with our truest desires. Trust in your aura, trust in your journey, and most importantly, trust in yourself as you continue to weave the vibrant tapestry of your life. Allow the mystery of existence to unfold, and may you find joy and fulfillment in each step of your never-ending journey.

FURTHER READING

HANDS OF LIGHT BY BARBARA BRENNAN
A foundational book on energy healing and the human energy field, offering insight into aura layers and chakras.

RADIANT HUMAN BY CHRISTINA LONSDALE
A modern exploration of aura photography and its meanings, providing practical approaches to understanding energy.

THE HIDDEN MESSAGES IN WATER BY MASARU EMOTO
A fascinating look into how energy affects the physical world, emphasizing the power of intention.

WAY OF THE PEACEFUL WARRIOR BY DAN MILLMAN
A transformative spiritual guide that integrates personal growth, mindfulness, and inner wisdom.

THE UPANISHADS (VARIOUS TRANSLATIONS)
Ancient Hindu scriptures exploring the concept of Prana, the life force energy surrounding all beings.

THE PĀLI CANON (BUDDHIST TEXTS)
These ancient scriptures describe the luminous aura and its connection to spiritual states.

ACKNOWLEDGMENTS

We acknowledge that Aura Weaver operates on the ancestral lands of the Muscogee Creek Nation, whose people were forcibly removed from this region. We honor the rich history, culture, and enduring presence of the Muscogee people and offer our deep respect to all Indigenous communities past, present, and future.

We would like to express our gratitude to our family, friends, and mentors who have supported us throughout this journey. To our clients and community, your trust and openness have been instrumental in helping us grow and evolve. Special thanks to our collaborators and contributors, Alberto Roman, Shana Robbins, Cristiana Valenti, Terp Vairin, Maggie Boyd, Shasta Zaring, and David Nichtern, who have enriched this project with their knowledge, creativity, and energy. A huge thank-you to Rhonda Mullen and Kate Zimmermann for providing invaluable guidance on writing our first book and to our RitualCravt family for providing a home for our aura explorations. And a special thank-you to the over thirty thousand individuals who have had an aura photo with us: we couldn't have done this without each of you.

ABOUT THE AUTHORS

DR. CHARLIE WATTS is a multidisciplinary academic, artist, and pelvic floor occupational therapist whose work bridges science, art, and metaphysical exploration. Focused on making birth safer and more inclusive, particularly in the American South, she combines her academic expertise with a passion for holistic care. Her internationally exhibited artwork—featured at the Harn Museum of Art, MOCA Cleveland, Vogue Italia, Saatchi Gallery in London, and the de Young Museum—explores the intersections of embodiment, energy, and the mystical. Dr. Watts offers compassionate, intuitive care at her Atlanta-based practice, supporting birthing individuals and patients with pelvic floor dysfunction. She lives in Atlanta with her husband and their cat, Josie Wales.

JUDAH ANDREWS is a lifelong performer of stage and circus. He is a voice actor, graphical artist, hip-hop dance teacher, hand balancer, and magician. He has performed in national productions across the country, for many blue chip clients including Coca-Cola, Cirque du Soleil, and Megan Thee Stallion. He has worked with several circus outreach programs for at-risk youth and those with special needs and has voiced dozens of audiobooks on Audible.com